11·11·77

POLICE STATE

RECENT BOOKS BY JULES ARCHER

China in the Twentieth Century

The Chinese and the Americans

Legacy of the Desert

The Russians and the Americans

Washington vs. Main Street: The Struggle
Between Federal and Local Power

Watergate: America in Crisis

POLICE STATE

Could It Happen Here?

by Jules Archer

Harper & Row, Publishers

New York   Hagerstown   San Francisco   London

FIRST EDITION

Library of Congress Cataloging in Publication Data
Archer, Jules.
   Police state.

   Bibliography: p.
   Includes index.
   SUMMARY: Discusses examples of major twentieth-
century police states and examines American history to
pursue the question, Could it happen here?
   1. Totalitarianism—Juvenile literature.
[1. Totalitarianism]   I. Title.
JC481.A587   321.9   76-58720
ISBN 0-06-020153-3
ISBN 0-06-020154-1 lib. bdg.

To the memory of
Len Archer
my beloved partner in the creation of
three sons and over fifty books

1981242

Contents

1

Democracies and Police States

During the administration of Richard M. Nixon (1969-1974), as this American President persisted in continuing an unpopular war in Vietnam, protesters staged huge antiwar demonstrations. Calling them Communist inspired, the President tried to ensure himself a second term in the White House by using the powers of his office to sabotage his political opponents.

In 1974 the American people became aware that, in pursuit of his objectives, the President and his aides had committed a number of crimes in violation of the Constitution.

They had authorized burglary. They had invaded citizens' privacy by ordering wiretapping and eavesdropping devices—"bugs"—planted in phones and walls, spying even on members of Congress. They had intercepted, opened and read private mail. They had illegally investigated and kept under surveillance citizens opposed to Nixon's policies.

They had used police agents to spy on and disrupt dissenting organizations. Government spies planted inside such groups had urged members to commit violent acts, to give the President an excuse to discredit all dissenters as terrorists out to destroy the nation.

When the press began to uncover and expose these and other unsavory administration secrets, Nixon and his aides urged everyone who could implicate the President to lie at court trials and Congressional hearings. They destroyed evidence, bribed arrested criminals to keep silent, and either ordered government agencies to cover up

1

their crimes or obstructed investigations into them.

The Nixon administration, said Washington columnist Joseph Kraft, was "the first criminal presidency in our country." Later Congressional investigations revealed, however, that previous Presidential administrations had also been guilty of violating the law, although not to the extent it was done in the Nixon years. At first, only the truth about the Nixon administration emerged. The President was compelled to resign to escape disgrace and prosecution; nothing like this had ever happened before in American history.

The American people had barely recovered from that shock when they were stunned by new disclosures in 1975. The government's two glorified intelligence agencies, the Federal Bureau of Investigation (FBI) and the Central Intelligence Agency (CIA), were revealed to have been breaking the law and violating the rights of American citizens for *many* years, throughout no less than six presidencies.

The FBI has authority to investigate violations of federal law, including interstate crime, kidnapping, espionage, sabotage, treason and threats to internal security. The CIA is authorized to gather, analyze and provide the National Security Council with *foreign* intelligence affecting our national security. Both agencies, however, were shown to have secretly exceeded their legal authority, often for political rather than the national security reasons they alleged.

Among their illegal acts had been wiretapping, burglary, bugging, opening mail, forging and concealing evidence, keeping dissenters under surveillance and checking on what they read, plotting the assassination of foreign leaders and plotting to overthrow other governments.

The trust of many Americans in their government was shaken. A 1975 poll by Cambridge Survey Research indicated that 68% of the American people were convinced that their leaders had been lying to them consistently.

"Indeed," observed Senator Philip A. Hart, "according to a recent national poll, over 60% of America's young people believe 'that the country is democratic in name only and run by special interests.' "

2

What is a democracy? Derived from a Greek word meaning "rule by the people," it characterized the early form of Greek government under which citizens governed themselves through elected representatives who made the nation's laws. Periodic free elections allow for political change, with a choice of parties and candidates. Individuals are secure in their personal liberties and in their right to disagree openly with the government. Courts are free to decide all cases purely on their merits.

Democracy is perhaps the most fragile of all political systems, precisely because it is more open, more vulnerable to criticism, more subject to disunity. The democratic free society is a government of laws, not men; its powers are divided, which often makes it less capable of swift and decisive action than a dictatorship. A democratic government is also limited in its exercise of power by laws protecting the rights of individuals, minorities, dissidents and local governing bodies. These laws are defined as civil liberties and guaranteed by a constitution, or spelled out in the nation's legal code.

What the Nixon administration, the FBI and the CIA did was in violation of the guarantees of our Constitution and its Bill of Rights —the first ten amendments. These guarantees protect Americans against having their democracy transformed into a police state.

The Bill of Rights guarantees your right to worship as you please, or not at all. It prevents the government from giving recognition to, or forcing you to pay taxes to support, any one religion. It protects your right to say whatever you want to whomever you want. It allows you to write and publish whatever you want, however unfavorable to the government. It gives you the right to read and listen to uncensored news, to find out what is happening in the country and the world.

"No mere administrative ruling that 'it is not in the best interests of the United States,' " observes historian Henry Steele Commager, "can silence freedom of speech or press."

The Bill of Rights entitles you to meet with any friends you care to, when and where you like. You may also gather with other citizens to protest government actions peacefully, or to demand changes in the law.

You are protected against "unreasonable searches and seizures," so that neither you, nor your home, nor your school locker, can be searched, or anything taken from you, without an official court warrant issued by a magistrate convinced by evidence that you may have violated the law.

If you're charged with a crime, you can't be required to give evidence against yourself—your protection against being tortured into signing a confession. You can't be jailed, executed or have your property confiscated, except through judicial proceedings in a court of law. You can't be held in jail indefinitely, but have the right to a "speedy and public trial by an impartial jury." You must be informed of the charges against you. Your accuser cannot remain secret, but must speak out in court where your lawyer can cross-examine him. You have the right to choose a lawyer to defend you, and to call witnesses in your behalf.

If a verdict goes against you, you theoretically have the right to appeal it to a higher court, all the way up to the Supreme Court. While awaiting the verdict of a lower or appeals court, you cannot be kept in jail by a judge's demand for excessive bail—the amount of money you must deposit with the court to assure that you will show up on the day of trial or sentence.

If you are found guilty, a judge cannot fine you a sum out of proportion to the seriousness of the offense. Like imposing a $10,000 fine for a parking violation if he doesn't like the way you wear your hair. Nor can he impose any "cruel and unusual" sentence, like ordering you whipped or tortured.

You cannot be tried in a place distant from the scene of the alleged law violation, but only in the state where it was committed. You cannot be brought to trial for any act you did before a law was passed making it illegal. Nor can the government pass laws barring any group you belong to from any of the full rights of citizenship.

The Constitution guarantees you those rights regardless of race, sex, religion, nationality or political beliefs. If you were born in the

4

United States or became a citizen through naturalization, you are also entitled to the right to vote without cost in all government elections, unless you are a convicted felon.

The Constitution and the Bill of Rights are the law of the land. Laws passed by Congress or by individual states cannot violate their provisions, although the Constitution can be amended. The Supreme Court has the last word on whether laws, government actions or court decisions are Constitutional. Any that are found to violate the Constitution or the Bill of Rights are declared unlawful and voided.

These safeguards of your liberties and rights, along with the process of free elections, are the essence of what democracy is all about. Not that the safeguards always work! Unscrupulous or ignorant government officials may violate the laws, persecuting Americans who oppose them, as the Nixon administration demonstrated perhaps more vividly than previous administrations. But if they are caught at it, as the Nixon administration was, they face a penalty of criminal prosecution or damage suits.

The Constitution and the Bill of Rights make it difficult for government officials to disregard the laws governing the rights of the people. But our government is far from perfect. We need to be ever watchful for abuses and miscarriages of justice. As John Philpot Curran, an Irish statesman, said in 1790, "Eternal vigilance is the price of liberty."

When we are vigilant, when we know our Constitutional rights and insist upon them, we have the force of the Constitution and the Supreme Court behind us—a power greater than that of any individual, even a President or government official.

3

A police state is the opposite of a democracy. It is a state in which a dictatorship imposed by a single ruler, party or group exercises total, rigid and repressive controls over the social, economic and political life of its citizens, usually by means of terror through a secret police force.

It is the nature of a dictatorial ruler to reach for absolute power, if this is obtainable. And even the mildest of dictators relies upon a secret police force, and the use of terror tactics, to paralyze any political opposition.

A citizen's rights in a police state are, in most cases, only whatever the dictatorship says they are. If there is a constitution, it is usually a mere piece of paper which exists for propaganda purposes. It does not regulate the law, nor in any way curb any actions the government wishes to take.

Similarly, a modern police state may often call itself a democracy without actually being one. The test of such a government is whether its power is absolute, unchecked by a freely elected legislature and an independent high court.

If you lived in a police state, you would have nothing to say about the people who had power over you, since you would not have the right to vote in a free election. You would be kept ignorant of what was going on, except for whatever the police state wanted you to know or believe. The press, radio, TV, movies and every other source of information would be under the control of government censors.

You would not be able to voice your opinion freely, associate with whomever you wished or go where you pleased, because of an army of secret police spying on the public. Their job would be to suppress dissent and criticism as treasonous, because it would endanger the security of the state by stirring revolt. It would be unsafe for you to be seen in the company of anyone who had fallen under the suspicion of the political police. You would be subject to arrest at any time, without a court warrant, even on false or inaccurate charges made by a spiteful neighbor. You could be held in jail or a concentration camp, without trial, for as long as the authorities deemed advisable. If you were given a trial, it might be a mock proceeding, with the outcome decided in advance. You might not even be told why you were in prison, nor allowed to notify anyone.

You might not be given any idea of when, if ever, you would be released. Conditions in jail might be so horrible that, in desperation, you would sign any confession in the hope of more lenient treatment. Or you might be tortured for information you were suspected of having about opponents of the government, even if these were members of your own family.

Amnesty International, a world organization dedicated to helping political prisoners, reported, "In over thirty countries torture is systematically applied to extract confessions, elicit information, penalize dissent and deter opposition to repressive governmental policy."

In a democracy you have freedom of movement, the liberty to change where you live and work, to travel abroad and to move to another country if you prefer. But a police state severely restricts your right of movement. You would generally need permission to change your place of residence and job. Most police states would not allow you to travel beyond their own borders or the borders of neighboring satellites, nor to move abroad. They prefer their citizens to remain unaware of the freedoms enjoyed in the democracies.

Thus the police state seeks as far as possible to remain a closed society. Foreign visitors are usually carefully limited as to where they can go and what they can see. Sensitive about world opinion, the police state does not want the repressive nature of its rule reported abroad.

In short, the police state denies its citizens both political rights and those freedoms known as civil liberties which we take for granted like the American air we breathe. We would not do so for long if the United States were to turn into a police state.

4

Throughout history authoritarian states have been far more common than democracies. Up to the mid-19th century, most kingdoms operated on police-state principles, with little regard for the rights of citizens.

"*I* am the state," Napoleon once said.

Government was run primarily for the benefit of the privileged classes, who wielded the power. It was not until revolutionary movements began sweeping around the world in 1848 that monarchs felt pressured to appease angry citizens by promising them constitutions and parliaments to protect their rights.

Even then it was not until the 20th century that those promises began to be kept. Many of Europe's despotic kingdoms became constitutional monarchies or republics. In some cases, however, they were replaced instead by police states.

During the past 60 years two principal kinds of police state have developed. On the political Left are the Communist states based on the ideas of Karl Marx and Friedrich Engels, two 19th-century intellectuals who believed that private ownership of property and business was basically corrupt because it led to the domination of the rich over the poor. Capitalism was doomed to crumble, they insisted, and would be replaced by a "dictatorship of the proletariat"—that is, the working classes.

The Communists have advocated taking all industry and agriculture out of private hands, to be operated instead as government enterprise, returning to workers and farmers the fruits of their own labor.

The first Communist state to appear was the Soviet Union, founded in Russia in 1917 by the Bolshevik party led by Nikolai Lenin. It was followed 32 years later by the Communist state in China, founded by Mao Tse-tung.

On the political Right are the Fascist states influenced by the ideas of Vilfredo Pareto, who rejected Marxist theory. Pareto argued that intellectuals were responsible for the mess the world was in, which could only be remedied by men of action through force and violence. Successful leadership, Pareto taught, consisted of the ability of bold leaders to seize opportunities at the right time.

The Fascists have advocated achieving national strength by unifying a country under a powerful dictator; by exterminating "inferior" ethnic groups to breed only a "master race"; and by waging war to win territory, treasure and glory.

The first Fascist state was the Italian dictatorship of Benito Mussolini in 1922. It was followed 11 years later by the Nazi police state led by Adolf Hitler in Germany. These Fascist states were run with the support of conservative, wealthy and powerful classes.

Both Communists and Fascists deny political freedom to the people they rule. Some political scholars, however, see a basic difference between the two systems.

"The plain fact," said an editorial in the liberal *Nation*, one of America's oldest weeklies, "is that the USSR and China—and Cuba

8

for that matter—are social revolutionary regimes. Good or bad, they *are* that. All arose from intolerable social conditions and all tried to correct those conditions. . . . Men like Marx, Lenin, Mao Tse-tung—Stalin, even—are not to be compared with Hitler and Mussolini, who never had a social philosophy, but were bent simply on rapine and conquest."

Not all scholars are willing to accept this distinction, but I find the perception both valid and significant. Thus I discuss the various dictatorships in this book not only in terms of the classic attributes of a police state—political bondage, denial of civil liberties, use of surveillance and violence—but in economic and social terms as well.

5

A recent survey indicated that 66 of the world's countries today, and 42% of the world's population, cannot be termed free. In late 1975 Daniel Patrick Moynihan, then American Ambassador to the UN, observed that the dwindling number of democracies represented at the UN were coming under increasing attacks from "totalitarian and Communist regimes and assorted ancient and modern despotisms."

"The dictatorships in Latin America, Africa and Asia," noted Robert M. Hutchins when he was Director of the Center for the Study of Democratic Institutions, "leave the Western world with an almost complete monopoly of self-government. Only Europe and North America make serious claims to democracy as we understand it."

In a world which each year sees more police states and fewer democracies, the possibility that our own country, too, might abandon democracy under the pressure of increasingly difficult economic problems cannot be ignored. Especially since many Americans today, perhaps because of a growing alienation from politics, are not as informed as they might be about different forms of government and economic systems.

Tomorrow's generation of voters will soon have the preservation of our democracy in their own hands. If they are unable to distinguish clearly between the characteristics of a democracy and those of a police state, they might be misled into supporting movements, candidates or legislation that could pave the way for an American dictatorship.

The conditions that breed police states are not unique to foreign countries. They are latent in any country, including our own. In recent years most Americans have come to realize that it is risky to trust one's government always to do the right thing, and to protect the liberties of the people.

"Liberty has never come from the Government," warned Woodrow Wilson. "Liberty has always come from the subjects of it. The history of liberty is a history of resistance."

In the pages that follow, we shall examine the conditions that brought about several police states, how power was seized by a dictatorship and what it is like to live under police states of both the Right and Left.

We need to recognize that police states may appeal to many people who are willing to forgo political freedom and civil liberties—especially if they have never enjoyed them—for what they believe are the more practical advantages of having adequate food, shelter and medical care. To help explain why, this book indicates some economic accomplishments of police states as seen by their own people, as well as their obvious shortcomings from a democratic point of view.

Especially in times of national crisis, it is vital that more millions of American voters learn to recognize the danger signals that warn us our way of life may be in peril. Their prompt political action could be the decisive factor in preventing the White House from becoming the tomb of democracy.

II

Hitler's Germany

In the wake of Germany's defeat in World War I, revolution erupted in many parts of the country. The German Empire came to an abrupt end in November 1918 when Kaiser Wilhelm fled to Holland for refuge. A struggle for power broke out between the Communist party, which wanted to establish a Communist Germany, and the Social Democratic party, which wanted a gradual, nonviolent abandonment of the German capitalist system.

The Social Democrats won out. They were supported by most Germans, who were frightened of Communism. Together with other non-Communist parties, the Social Democrats formed a new democratic government called the Weimar Republic.

But German citizens were dismayed when the Weimar Republic admitted German guilt for starting the war by signing the punitive Versailles Treaty that forced Germany to pay reparations for war damages and the cost of Allied occupation troops. The treaty also transferred German territory to France, Belgium and Poland, stripped Germany of colonies and its merchant fleet, and forbade German rearmament.

Adolf Hitler, an Austrian-born war veteran, denounced the "traitors" of the Weimar Republic. He lumped them bitterly with all "enemies of the Fatherland" he considered guilty of its ruin, including the vengeful Allies, the Communists and the Jews, whom he blamed for keeping Germans helpless and poor. He would sweep them all aside, he vowed, and restore Germany to its former glory.

Failure had dogged Hitler's early efforts to "be somebody."

11

Spurned as an artist, he had spent five humiliating years (1905–1910) in Vienna shoveling snow, beating carpets, painting houses and working as a railroad porter. It was the fault of the "rich Jews" of Vienna, he fumed, who were out to enslave the world!

He had greeted the outbreak of World War I in 1914 with relief, enlisting in the German infantry. What an exciting thing war was— so filled with dramatic violence! Fighting courageously, he was decorated for bravery and won promotion to corporal. Germany's defeat found him hospitalized by an attack of poison gas.

A brooding Hitler grew convinced that Germans needed someone like him to lift them out of their postwar misery. Everyone knew that it was the destiny of Germans to be the "master race." All they needed was a strong leader—a Hitler. Turning to politics, he modeled himself on the example of a self-appointed messiah he greatly admired—the strutting, jackbooted Benito Mussolini of Italy.

Joining the National Socialist German Workers' (Nazi) party, he soon rose to leadership by making fanatical anti-Semitic speeches in Munich beer halls. The Jews were to blame for all of Germany's troubles, Hitler screamed. Germany's defeat had been a plot engineered by international Jewish bankers! Communism was *also* a Jewish plot! A Nazi regime would keep German blood pure of any Jewish taint—unlike the Weimar Republic, which had become "mongrelized." Germans must destroy the Jews, must become masters of the "Jew-ridden lower races." He meant the English, French, Poles and Russians.

Anti-Nazis who sought to challenge his wild tirades were quickly clubbed into silence by Hitler's Storm Troopers, the police arm of the Nazis, who were cheered on by his fascinated listeners. Many Germans, confused and bewildered, hungered for a strong leader to replace the Kaiser. They sought a messiah who seemed to know what was wrong, and how to restore Germany once more to its place in the sun.

Hitler represented himself as the embodiment of the popular German will, which he considered reflected by the lower middle class. Although he used the terms "Socialist" and "Workers" in the name of his party, they were only bait to lure workers away from the Social Democrats and Communists. Many industrialists approved of his

Storm Troopers' bloody street attacks on Communists, and secretly responded to Nazi appeals for funds.

By the end of 1920 the Nazis had enlisted 6,000 members, and had organized 100,000 sympathizers into a "Citizens' Defense." England protested that this paramilitary force violated the Versailles Treaty ban on German rearmament. The Weimar Republic ordered the Citizens' Defense dissolved. Hitler was delighted. What a propaganda opportunity he now had to harass the government as antipatriotic!

"We will incite the people, and not only incite, we will lash them to a frenzy!" he told his fellow Nazis. "We will preach struggle against this parliamentary breed, which will not cease until either Germany has been totally ruined or one day a man with an iron skull appears to show the nation some action!" And who else would the man with the iron skull be, of course, except Adolf Hitler?

In 1923 when the German economy collapsed, the Nazis made their move. Runaway inflation sent the price of a pound of meat soaring from 4 marks to 2 billion. Shocked Germans found their savings wiped out, their insurance policies and pensions worthless. Suffering grew intense as prices for food, clothing and rent soared. Factories were forced to shut down, throwing millions out of work. Hitler ranted. That miserable Weimar Republic! What a helpless, hopeless, hapless excuse for a government—doing nothing while Germans starved!

The Communist party worked for a general uprising. So did the Nazis. On November 8, 1923, Hitler led over 3,000 Storm Troopers in a "putsch" to take over Munich and the government of the state of Bavaria. Government forces crushed the revolt. Hitler was flung into jail, sentenced to five years. He served only nine months, however—in considerable comfort, thanks to powerful and wealthy supporters who pulled strings.

His "martyrdom" by the unpopular Weimar Republic made him a sympathetic figure in the eyes of some Germans, giving him national prominence. He had used his time in prison to write a book of propaganda, *Mein Kampf* (*My Battle*), which quickly became the bible of Nazism. Didn't Darwin's theory of the survival of the fittest, Hitler demanded, prove the Nazi policy of "might makes right"?

"Those who want to live, let them fight," he wrote, "and those who do not want to fight, in this world of eternal struggle, do not deserve to live." He advocated German territorial expansion in the east, to eventually swallow Russia and create *Lebensraum*—living space—for the German "master race." "This soil exists for the people which possesses the force to take it," he declared. And after eastern Europe and Russia? World conquest would make Germany "lord of the earth."

There would be no "democratic nonsense" when Hitler became dictator of a Third Reich. Jews, Communists and Slavs would be destroyed as "lower human types," to prevent their marriage to "Aryans" (blond Nordic types) and the "mongrelization" of "pure Aryan blood" by children of mixed parentage. It was proper to destroy them because "all who are not of good race in this world are chaff."

Mein Kampf put Germans on notice that Adolf Hitler intended to end democracy in Germany, make himself dictator, conquer Europe and the world, and eliminate millions of people he hated. Those who followed him with enthusiasm and devotion were not kept in the dark as to his intentions. But many supported him simply because he seemed to offer a realistic escape from the miseries they were suffering in postwar Germany.

2

By the time Hitler emerged from prison, the Nazi party and its press had been banned. He was forbidden to speak in public. What a democracy! he sneered. Worse, from his point of view, the Weimar Republic, aided by loans from America, had succeeded in getting inflation under control and the currency stabilized. The economy recovered rapidly.

Hitler doggedly set to work building the Nazi party underground with the aid of funds from industrialists. From only 27,000 members in 1925, the Nazis grew to a once-more-legal party of 178,000 four years later. His Brownshirts, special troops recruited mainly from the lowest elements of street brawlers, terrorized neighborhoods.

14

Since his putsch had failed, he decided to seek power through parliamentary means, at least at first. This meant winning elections to install as many Nazis as possible within the German parliament, the Reichstag.

The elections of 1925 came as a shock to Hitler. Of all the parties in the race, the Nazis came in a miserable seventh, with only 285,000 votes—less than a sixth of the votes polled by the Communist party. Conditions had improved so much under the Weimar Republic that now only one German in 94 wanted to see Adolf Hitler in power.

Hitler intensified his propaganda with funds supplied by a number of barons of industry. But the Nazis continued to do poorly at the polls until the world depression occurred, triggered by the American stock-market crash of 1929. German factories were forced to shut down, leaving 6 million people jobless. Discontent flared anew. Many angry Germans joined the ranks of the Nazis. By 1930, with 16% of Germans unemployed, the Nazi party received a staggering 6,400,000 votes. It won 107 out of 608 seats in the Reichstag, making it the second-largest party in the nation. Nazi propaganda, shrewdly churned out by Joseph Goebbels, had convinced more and more Germans that only Hitler could rescue them from disaster.

By 1932 the Communists had become the third-largest party and continued to grow rapidly. Nazi Storm Troopers, known as the SA, fought them savagely in bloody street battles. Leaders of the weak Weimar Republic felt helpless to prevent these disorders. The military was fearful that any attempt to suppress parties of either the Right or the Left, or both, would bring on civil war. The Weimar constitution, moreover, made no provisions for coping with dissension.

Hitler put the Nazi party's propaganda apparatus into high gear. Such huge, stirring parades! Mass meetings lit by searchlights and torches! Flaming speeches orchestrated with storms of applause, roars of "Heil, Hitler!" Exciting clashes to punish anyone who dared shout opposition! The German people were impressed. Emotions were taken by storm.

Hitler appealed to lower-middle-class Germans who were tired of the floundering Weimar Republic and wanted a stronger, authoritarian state. Inflaming their fears of growing Communist influence, he portrayed himself as the German scourge of Communism. If they would swear fealty to him, he would lead them out of the wilderness. Jobs for the jobless! A future for the idle, restless youth of Germany! A new strong Fatherland! No more reparations payments to the Allies! Repudiation of the Versailles Treaty! Destruction of the Jewish "money barons" and confiscation of their wealth! No more Weimar nonsense about equal rights for women—restoration of women's natural function as mothers and guardians of the home!

Millions of Germans began to believe that Hitler was, indeed, Germany's messiah whose hour had come. Was he not the people's champion? Did he not defy the government that permitted the "little Germans" to suffer in hopeless misery?

Some German army generals saw Hitler as a strong man who could free them from the shackles of Versailles. They agreed to give secret military training to his SA troops. Hitler also held secret meetings with leading industrialists all over Germany. Upon his reassurances that when the Nazis took power, he would jail or destroy all radicals, smash labor unions, prevent strikes and allow unlimited profits for big business, large contributions flowed into Nazi coffers.

Some prominent supporters who grew to know Hitler well, however, became apprehensive about his sanity. He made wild utterances. Vowing a war of revenge against the Allies, he declared he would wage it personally—without generals! If it were lost, he would drag down the whole world in flames! Germany would never again surrender! Then, like an orchestra playing the crashing finale of a Wagnerian opera, he began humming the dramatic score of *Götterdämmerung*.

Hitler's chief obstacle to power was the aging President of Germany, Field Marshal Paul von Hindenburg. The highly respected war hero and elder statesman resisted all hints that he name Hitler the next Chancellor, or Prime Minister, of Germany. He distrusted the fiery Nazi leader as a madman bent on plunging the nation into another disastrous war.

But the economic depression persisted. Six million Germans were

16

jobless, the middle classes faced ruin, farmers were unable to meet mortgage payments. The government was stricken with paralysis as the Reichstag wrangled over party squabbles. In the elections of March 1932 Hindenburg failed to win a majority of the vote, receiving just over 49%. Hitler netted 30% and the Communist leader 13%.

This necessitated a runoff election between the three top candidates in April. Hitler mounted another whirlwind campaign. He even appealed for the vote of single girls by pledging, "In the Third Reich every German girl will find a husband!" But Hindenburg increased his vote to 53%, winning another term as President. Hitler's vote increased to almost 37%. The Communists dropped to 10%, indicating that almost four times as many Germans preferred the Nazis to the Communists. Over a third of Germany wanted Hitler as President.

The Weimar government grew alarmed at rumors of an impending military putsch by Hitler's 400,000 Storm Troopers under Captain Ernst Roehm. The SA, which had beaten up and murdered opponents of the Nazis and smashed their meetings, was outlawed. Hitler simply ordered the Storm Troopers to take off their uniforms. They would continue operating underground until he could force Hindenburg to appoint him Chancellor. But Hindenburg contemptuously refused to consider Hitler for any post more important than chief of the post office.

The chancellorship went to diplomat Franz von Papen, leader of the small Nationalist party. Stung, the Nazis continued attacking the Weimar Republic as "the Jews' republic."

Seeking to neutralize Nazi opposition, Hindenburg's son made a deal with Hitler. The Storm Troopers would be allowed to return to uniform if they renewed their campaign of terror against the Communists throughout Germany. Hitler promptly agreed. The legal police and army, secretly sympathetic with the Nazis, did not interfere with the new street battles.

In an attempt to show their own power, the Communists called a general work strike. But most trade unions refused to cooperate, and the strike collapsed.

On July 31, 1932, the Nazis won 230 seats in the Reichstag, making them the largest party (although not by a majority), followed by the Social Democrats with 133 and the Communists with 89. Hitler's chief aide, Hermann Goering, was elected presiding officer. Hitler pressed his demands to be named Chancellor, and to have Nazis appointed to positions of authority throughout Germany.

"Once we have the power we will never give it up," Joseph Goebbels told his fellow Nazis in private. "They will have to carry our dead bodies out of the ministries."

Hindenburg continued to resist Hitler's demands. Using a political trick, Goering dissolved the Reichstag once more, forcing still another election. But to the Nazis' dismay, this time they lost 33 seats while the Communists added 11. Papen was replaced as Chancellor by General Kurt von Schleicher.

The Nazis were disheartened by Hitler's failure to win control of Germany by a parliamentary victory. Their financial aid was cut off by industrialists who now considered him an unprofitable investment. The party teetered on bankruptcy. There was a party revolt against Hitler's leadership, but he crushed it.

The new Chancellor, Schleicher, appealed for popular support of the Weimar Republic by ordering increases in wages and relief benefits, price controls on coal and meat, and confiscation of large agricultural estates for division among 25,000 peasant families. Alarmed by what seemed to be a new anticapitalist policy, one powerful group of wealthy Germans secretly sent Papen to Hitler to propose a deal. Would the Nazis agree to join forces with the Nationalist party in dumping Schleicher's regime and replacing it with a Hitler-Papen coalition? The bribe: Hitler would become Chancellor, and the businessmen behind Papen would pay off Nazi debts and refill the party's treasury.

Delighted, Hitler promptly agreed. The German army high command, fearing the growing influence of the Communists, also decided to support the Nazis as a lesser risk. Their decision tipped the scales in Hitler's favor. Pressure was put on Hindenburg to name Hitler Chancellor. On January 30, 1933, the aging, ailing President reluctantly summoned the Nazi leader. Would Herr Hitler be willing to try to form a new government?

18

3

So, without firing a shot, the former ne'er-do-well of Vienna took control of the destinies of 60 million Germans. What a celebration! In an endless torchlight parade, tens of thousands of jackbooted Storm Troopers flung up a forest of hands in the adulatory Nazi salute to their leader. He reviewed them proudly from the balcony of the Chancellery.

Hitler had no intention of sharing power with either Papen, his wealthy supporters or the army. Within five hours of taking office, he moved to make himself exclusive master of Germany by once more dissolving the Reichstag and calling for new elections. With all the machinery of government in his power, he could easily manipulate the elections and rig a huge victory at the polls. That would give him the exclusive right to make key appointments throughout Germany, in effect turning the nation into a Nazi dictatorship.

First he called a secret meeting of several dozen of Germany's leading industrial magnates, appealing for big contributions to a new Nazi election campaign. What, they demanded, was in it for them? Hitler spelled out what their money would buy. Unions controlled and forbidden to strike. Big business free to run as it wished, without interference. Germany's Communists destroyed. Huge armaments orders for the munition makers, in defiance of the Versailles Treaty ban on rearmament. Best of all—an end to democracy in Germany.

Ah, yes, but if he lost the election? In that case, he assured them, it would be the last Germany would ever hold. He would still retain power "by the other means . . . with weapons."

The industrialists approved his plan enthusiastically. Munitions tycoon Gustav Krupp expressed his "gratitude" for the cooperative attitude of the new Chancellor.

Goering, who had been made Minister of Police for the state of Prussia, announced that documents had been captured in Berlin indicating that the Communists were planning revolution. To "prove" it he gave secret orders to the SA. Five days before the scheduled election, SA leader Carl Ernst took a squad of Storm Troopers into the Reichstag building and soaked the interior with gasoline and inflammable chemicals. Then a demented Dutch Communist named Marinus van der Lubbe, who had been arrested, was sent into the empty building with matches and encouraged to use them. Two minutes after he entered the Reichstag, it burst into flame in a dozen places. Goering later boasted privately, "The only one who really knows about the Reichstag is I—because *I* set it on fire!"

But publicly he roared, "This is the beginning of the Communist revolution! We must not wait a minute. We will show no mercy. Every Communist official must be shot where he is found. Every Communist deputy must be strung up this very night!"

Hitler quickly persuaded Hindenburg to sign an emergency decree called "The Protection of the People and the State." Designated "a defensive measure against Communist acts of violence," it suspended seven sections of the Weimar constitution that guaranteed individual and civil liberties.

Hitler now had the power to arrest and lock up anyone he professed to suspect of treasonable intentions. Storm Troopers were permitted to violate the privacy of postal, telegraphic and phone communications, break into homes and search them, and confiscate any records. In a wild night of Nazi terror, March 1, 1933, truckloads of Storm Troopers raided homes and offices all over Germany. Communist deputies, trade unionists, Left-wing journalists and other anti-Nazis were dragged off to jail, where they were beaten and tortured. All anti-Nazi papers were shut down. All anti-Nazi meetings banned.

The German middle class and peasantry, thrown into panicky fear of a "Communist takeover," were urged to vote Nazi as the only way in which Germany could be "saved." The ballot was still ostensibly secret, but rumors now spread that the Nazis had ways of detecting everyone who voted against them. Such information would be passed on to the Nazi secret police—the dreaded Gestapo.

Despite this campaign of terror and intimidation, the Nazis still won only 17 million votes—44%—while even now the Communists received 5 million—12%. Papen's little Nationalist party, however, won just enough votes; these—combined with the Nazi vote—gave Hitler the slim majority he needed to stay in power in the new

Reichstag. But it was not enough to let him claim a mandate for establishing a dictatorship.

Hitler decided that he had not intimidated the German people sufficiently. "The ordinary man in the street respects nothing but brutal strength and ruthlessness," he said. "Women, too. For that matter, women and children. The people need wholesome fear. They *want* to fear something. They want someone to frighten them and make them shudderingly submissive."

To gain that power he proposed the "Enabling Act"—a "Law for Removing the Distress of People and Reich." It would give him dictatorial powers for four years, entitling him to draft any laws he liked without regard for the constitution or the Reichstag. He sent the bill to the Opera House, where the Reichstag had met since the fire, demanding its passage.

Goering surrounded the Opera House with thousands of armed Storm Troopers. All Communist members were refused admission. "Pass the law—or bleed!" the SA roared in unison. The frightened parliament passed Hitler's Enabling Act by a vote of 441 to 84. Many of those who voted nay were subsequently arrested, and some were killed.

With this act Hitler became dictator of Germany at last, on March 23, 1933. The country was not to have another free election for the twelve years of his rule by terror. The Germans had ostensibly escaped Communist revolution by accepting Fascist counterrevolution. Each four years afterward a rubber-stamp Reichstag would automatically renew the Enabling Act that gave Hitler his legal pretext for dictatorship.

Hitler made no secret, however, of his contempt for "the voice of the people." In *Mein Kampf* he had scoffed at "the Jewish-Democratic idea of blind worship of majorities." Should not the masses be content to obey those set apart by nature to rule over them? That elite of born leaders who could govern by the sheer force of personality and willpower?

Many Germans did, in fact, seem more comfortable at finding themselves once again under the autocratic rule that had been a national tradition. The youth of Germany were blindly worshipful of the new Fuehrer (leader) who promised them an exciting, vibrant future that included mastery of the world. They flung up swastika-banded arms in proud Nazi salutes as they marched by him in review, roaring, *"Sieg heil!"* ("Victory—hail!")

Hitler lost no time in dissolving all state governments. Anti-Nazi officials were turned out of office, replaced by obedient Nazi governors. All other political parties were declared illegal and forced to dissolve. All unions were merged into a Nazi-controlled New Labor Front, under Robert Ley. Storm Troopers raided trade-union offices, arresting officials who "may hypocritically declare their devotion to the Fuehrer as much as they like," as Ley said, "but it is better that they should be in prison." All strikes were outlawed "to restore absolute leadership to the natural leader of a factory"—that is, the employer.

Hitler's wealthy backers had been repaid.

Storm Troopers dominated the streets of Germany without opposition, beating up, torturing or kicking to death anyone they disliked. They assaulted Jewish shopkeepers, crippled suspected Leftists, broke into homes to hang anti-Nazis in their kitchens. Some outraged church leaders protested.

"I won't be a spoilsport to any of my men," Hitler replied. "If I demand the utmost of them, I must also permit them to let off steam as *they* please—not as it suits a lot of elderly church hens. My lads are no angels, God knows. Nor are they expected to be. I've no use for goody-goodies!"

Joseph Goebbels headed the "Ministry for Popular Enlightenment and Propaganda," which was given control of all German radio, newspapers and publishing houses. He constantly sounded the alarm of a "Jewish conspiracy" to rule the world. But never fear! That destiny belonged only to the German "master race." If any German had any doubt as to what was right, "right is what is good for the German people." *Sieg heil!* (Behind this propaganda front Nazi party members were assured that only those elite Germans wearing swastika armbands were the *real* supermen who would wield all the power.)

Goebbels brainwashed Germans into believing that Hitler had brought them *"genuine* democracy and equality," because the "real

22

will of the people" now prevailed through the "discipline and order" that had ended civil liberties and political divisions. Day after day the language was twisted and stood on its head until only the most strong-minded Germans were able to distinguish fact from fiction.

To siphon off discontent, the German people were given a scapegoat for all their disappointments—the Jews. Frustrated Germans were encouraged to vent their rage by beating up Jews, and destroying or plundering their property. Laws were passed discriminating against Jews in a hundred different ways. Even Hitler's ally, Italian dictator Mussolini, was appalled.

"I do not want to fight world Jewry," he told Goering, "or a world that will sympathize with the Jews whom you are murdering."

Worried by the lawlessness of the Nazi regime, Papen made a speech suggesting that perhaps the time had come to restore "right and justice." Goering ordered news of the speech suppressed.

In the space of just one year Hitler had overthrown the Weimar Republic, destroyed democracy, abolished all political parties except the Nazis, wrested power from the German states, ended all civil liberties, swept Jews out of public life, wrecked the labor-union movement, established total censorship and clamped a personal dictatorship on the German people.

Hitler, many Germans said proudly, was a man of action. Unlike the feeble Weimar leaders, he got things done!

4

Enforcing Hitler's decrees were the regular police and Gestapo secret police under Goering, Hitler's own SS political police guard under Heinrich Himmler, and the SA Storm Troopers under Ernst Roehm. Goering, Himmler and Roehm vied with each other for power in a confusion of private empires, private armies and private intelligence services. This pyramid of terror alarmed even those Germans who professed themselves loyal Nazis.

Trouble loomed with Hitler's wealthy backers when Roehm insisted that the Nazis, having destroyed the Left, should now destroy the Right. To exercise total power over Germany and justify the "Socialist" portion of the Nazi name, Roehm argued, big business and finance, the aristocracy, the big landlords and the Prussian generals all had to be regimented.

"I think, my dear Ernst," Hitler told him coldly, "you take too seriously the slogans we used to gain power."

The army's generals were infuriated by Roehm's attempt to oust them and take over the army with his SA. They insisted that Hitler act to crush Roehm and his Storm Troopers.

On June 29, 1934, Hitler launched a bloodbath known as "the night of the long knives." Roehm and hundreds of his SA leaders were seized and shot. Hitler also used the occasion to get rid of others who had opposed him, such as the former Chancellor, General Schleicher, who was murdered with his wife.

One month later Hitler had his reward when President Hindenburg died. The army now agreed to let Hitler combine the offices of President and Chancellor, swearing loyalty to him as Commander-in-Chief of the Armed Forces. His dictatorship was complete. He was now free not only to restructure and regiment every German institution along totalitarian lines, but also to use the army to capture all of Europe for Fascism.

"There will be no more revolutions in Germany for the next thousand years!" he told a roaring mass of 200,000 party officials gathered in Nuremberg in September 1934, under 21,000 swastika flags at a spectacular floodlit rally. But Hitler's thousand-year Reich was destined to last only a dozen years.

In 1935 a new penal code established punishment, regardless of prior law, for any act against "wholesome popular sentiment." Wholesome popular sentiment? That meant whatever Hitler disapproved. Judges were ordered to decide cases "as they believed the Fuehrer would himself decide them." In effect, Hitler abolished the existing code of laws and established his own personal set of laws by decree.

Judges who tried to administer impartial justice were dismissed for "political unreliability." Any accused defendant given too light a sentence in the opinion of the Gestapo was seized and spirited off to a concentration camp for extralegal Nazi punishment. Many were kept there without trial.

Gestapo torture was both physical and mental. Many prisoners were given the choice of betraying anti-Nazi friends or suffering torture and sealing the death warrants of their wives and children. There was no appeal from a Gestapo decision.

No one was safe at home from the listening ears of the secret police. Diplomats, officials and private citizens were driven to meet in public parks, or to whisper in bathrooms with the water running, to escape electronic eavesdroppers.

The Nuremberg Laws of September 1935 deprived Jews of citizenship and forbade them to marry "Aryans." Obliged to wear yellow armbands for identification, they were often barred from food shops, drugstores and hotels, and forced to depend for their needs on sympathetic non-Jews who dared help them secretly.

In November 1938, when a Jewish youth shot a German Embassy official in Paris, Hitler used the incident as a pretext for organized riots. "The Jews must be shown that they cannot interfere with the Fuehrer," he screamed. "Step on them like vermin!" All over Germany Jewish homes, shops and synagogues were plundered and burned. Thousands of Jews were dragged from their homes in the middle of the night and shot, while 25,000 were thrown into concentration camps.

In a final touch of irony, Goering fined German Jewry a billion marks for "causing" the disorders! This was too much for America's President Franklin D. Roosevelt, who recalled the American ambassador from Germany to express his indignation.

5

Living in Hitler's police state as a German, you might easily have been taken in, at least at first, by the professed patriotism and idealism of the Nazi movement. Those thrilling rallies with their outdoor spectacles portraying Hitler as the messiah for whom the German people were waiting impatiently! Hitler's spellbinding portrayals of Germans as "the master race"—superior to all other races in the world!

It would have been hard not to be impressed by the great increase in German prestige that had followed his transformation of a weak and troubled nation into a united, organized, powerful state. Your doubts about him might have been offset by fears of the class warfare preached by the Communists. Wasn't that a "Jewish plot" to divide Germans against each other?

Your idealism would have been appealed to by the Nazi slogan, "The Common Interest Before Self!" If you loved your country, shouldn't you accept the sacrifices demanded by the Fuehrer? Surrender of personal freedom? Regimentation? Guns instead of butter? Long, hard work for subsistence wages?

If you were convinced by the barrage of Nazi propaganda that "enemies of the state" were everywhere, why would you quarrel with the law that forbade criticism of the state—even in conversation between husband and wife? "There is no such thing," said Robert Ley, "as privacy for the individual in National Socialist Germany." Maybe you wouldn't have agreed to spy on your neighbor. But how could you be sure he hadn't agreed to spy on you? There were Gestapo spies in every neighborhood, recruited with either money or threats. So you would prudently have held your tongue. Otherwise the Gestapo might pound on your door in the middle of the night to drag you and your family to jail or a concentration camp.

One typist repeated a joke about Hitler to other young women in her office. She was reported, arrested and sentenced to two years' imprisonment for "malicious vilification."

As a religious Catholic or Protestant, you might have been upset when the Nazis arrested thousands of priests, nuns and pastors who resisted Hitler's attempt to transform the church in Germany into a pagan religion of leader worship. The Nazis literally sought to replace the Bible with *Mein Kampf*, the cross with the swastika— the "twisted cross." Yet Bishop Marahrens of Hanover required all pastors to swear a personal oath of allegiance to the Fuehrer. "The National Socialist conception of life," he advised his flock, "is obligatory upon German Christians as well."

Having suffered through years of unemployment and hard times, you would have been grateful for the jobs Hitler provided through vast public works—government buildings, housing, expressways— and a huge armaments industry, built in defiance of the Versailles Treaty. So what if you were underpaid and not allowed to strike? Weren't you and other workers held up to the nation as glorious

26

examples of German patriotism, contributing to "national unity"?

You might not have questioned the new censorship of all press and radio news. "It is the State's duty," Goebbels explained, "not to . . . be led astray by the will-o'-the-wisp of so-called 'freedom of the press.' . . . It must keep control of that instrument . . . and place it at the service of the State." When audiences hissed at the insipid Nazi-approved films moviemakers were limited to producing, an angry Nazi official threatened reprisals against such "treasonable behavior."

You would have been able to read only those books, see only those works of art, hear only that music, which were certified "pure" for Germans by Goebbels's Propaganda Ministry. *Verboten* (forbidden) books were burned in bonfires. "Un-German" works of art were destroyed. The president of the Reich Theater Chamber explained how a true Nazi felt when someone mentioned the word "culture":

"It makes me want to reach for my revolver," he said.

Hitler, who had been a school dropout at age 13, reshaped German education in his own image. "We shall bestow upon the broad mass of the lowest class the blessings of illiteracy," he told an intimate seriously. He explained: "My system of education is a harsh one. Weakness must be stamped out. . . . A violent, masterful, dauntless, cruel younger generation—that is my aim. . . . I want no intellectual instruction. Knowledge spells perdition to my young people. . . . I want them to learn to conquer the fear of death by undergoing the severest ordeals."

As a student you would have been given the slogan "Believe, Obey, Fight!" Principal topics for study were Nazi history, the ideas of the Fuehrer, and "the need for, and nature of, racial purity." But you would have spent most of your time in gymnastics, field sports, rallies and marches. "Marching," you would have been taught, "is more important than studying."

To be "properly educated" as a girl, you would have been required to complete long cross-country marches, perform a flying forward roll and execute a nine-foot dive into cold water. But while boys were trained for military service, you would have been prepared to become a housewife and mother. To encourage an increased birthrate—more soldiers for the Fuehrer!—you would have been drafted for a year of

27

domestic service as unpaid help for mothers with large families.

The Nazi police state worked to channel your loyalty away from your family. Patriotic duty required you to report any disloyal statements by your parents. You would have been expected, if a boy, to join the Hitler Youth at age 10, taking an oath "to the savior of our country, Adolf Hitler," pledging, "I am willing and ready to give up my life for him, so help me God!" If a girl, you would have taken a similar oath in the Association of German Girls. The regimentation of youth was made attractive by military-style uniforms, marching songs and parades with flapping swastika banners.

Adults were also regimented under a Strength Through Joy Association. It filled their lives with state activities outside the home, especially factory sports, walking tours through Germany and other cheap mass holidays designed to make Germans "physically fit" for the hardships of wars being planned.

A wry German joke asked, "What is the ideal German family? It's a family in which the father is a member of the Nazi party, the mother belongs to the Association of Nazi Women, the daughter to the Association of German Girls, the son to the Hitler Youth—and they all meet once a year at the Nazi Congress in Nuremberg!"

As Hitler's plans for a new world war developed, with more and more German men leaving the country to fight, acute labor shortages developed. The Nazis drafted all women under 25 for agricultural work and factory labor. If you had been a Labor Service girl, single or married, you would have been instructed that it was an act of patriotism to bear a child fathered by an SS man "for the Fuehrer," to replace Germans falling in battle. "You can't all get a husband," one party official told an audience of Labor Service girls, "but you can all be mothers."

If you had been one of those Germans enjoying a guaranteed job, inexpensive holidays and the pride of "being on a winning team," you might have felt fiercely loyal to the police state that made it all possible. Weren't you cared for by the Nazi party? Wasn't it ready to help loyal citizens like you if you became sick or unemployed, or otherwise got into difficulty? Why should the horrors perpetrated by the Gestapo affect you? You might fear the Gestapo, but it wasn't *you* who was being tortured!

28

"The lives of my friends . . . were lightened and brightened by National Socialism as they knew it," recalled a former small-town Nazi party member of the days before World War II. "And they look back at it now . . . as the best time of their lives. . . . There were jobs and job security, summer camps for the children and the Hitler Youth to keep them off the streets. . . . So things went better."

6

Having conquered his enemies at home, in 1938 Hitler set out to fulfill his dreams of world conquest. "Strength alone constitutes the right to possess," he had written in *Mein Kampf*. His powerful Nazi army, built in secret, marched across one border after another until between 1938 and 1942 Austria, Czechoslovakia, Poland, Denmark, Norway, Holland, Belgium, France and all of eastern Europe lay beneath the German heel. Utilizing food, wealth, armed forces and manpower of those conquered lands, he unleashed his armies against the Slavic people he hated as a "mongrel, subhuman race"—the Russians.

Millions of men and women in territories conquered by the Nazis were seized on the streets and deported to Germany in boxcars, along with prisoners of war, for slave labor in factories, fields and mines. Most were terrorized, beaten, starved, often left to die for lack of clothing, shelter or rest. Forced to work up to 16 hours a day on a diet of watery soup and black bread, those who collapsed or protested were executed.

As the Nazi war machine ground on, millions of Jews, Russians, Poles and anti-Nazis were destroyed in mass executions by Himmler's SS organization in extermination camps. At Minsk in 1941, Himmler ordered a hundred prisoners executed in his presence simply as a demonstration of Nazi efficiency.

Two years later, at a military ceremony in Posen (now called Poznan), he told SS generals he decorated, "Most of you must know what it means when 100 dead bodies are lying side by side, or 500 or 1,000. To have endured this and at the same time . . . to have preserved one's decency—that is what has made us hard. . . . We must be honest, decent, loyal and comradely to members of our own race, and to no one else."

The freezing boxcars used to ship victims to concentration camps in midwinter were often jammed so full that upon arrival three fourths of the prisoners were already icy corpses. Those who survived were tattooed on the arm with numbers, worked mercilessly, humiliated and beaten like animals.

Many of those tortured and killed in the German concentration camps were Germans. "When the SS struck, you dared not strike back," recalled a German Communist prisoner, Mrs. Buber-Neumann. "When the SS bullied and insulted, you had to keep your mouth shut and never answer back. You had lost all human rights."

The guards chosen were often sadists who enjoyed the power of torturing people. "I will never forget the faces of my torturers," said one survivor, a teenage girl. "I will never forget that place where the walls were spattered with human flesh and blood, where the torturers amused themselves by seeing who could produce the loudest screams."

Millions of Jews from Germany, Russia and all over Europe were massacred in gas chambers, then fed into crematory ovens, to fulfill Hitler's vow, "They will be killed like flies!" He enjoyed watching films of mass murders in the concentration camps of Auschwitz, Belsen, Buchenwald and Dachau.

Nazi doctors used camp prisoners for ghastly experiments. To see how long and high a flier could go without an oxygen mask, 800 prisoners were sealed in closed cars from which the air was pumped until they were asphyxiated. To see how long shot-down fliers could survive in the English Channel, 600 people were kept in below-zero seawater until they perished. To test experimental drugs, 2,000 Polish priests were injected with disease germs. Half of them died.

The horrors of Nazi conquest were endless. Some prisoners were gassed in order to use their tattooed skins as lampshades. Some with perfect teeth were killed to use their skulls as paperweights. Himmler ordered that captured Russian commissars should be killed without damage to their skulls, as he wanted them for "scientific research" on the "subhuman species of Jewish-Bolshevik commissars."

The concentration camps all over Nazi-occupied Europe were

operated by SS officers who, with their wives and children, lived comfortably in spacious homes with lovely gardens beneath skies black with smoke bearing human ashes. It was they, as Hitler's elite political police, who carried out the extermination of 7 million concentration-camp prisoners, and who held 10 million Europeans enslaved.

"I pray for the defeat of my country," said German Pastor Dietrich Bonhoeffer in a secret meeting. "It is only through this defeat that we will be able to atone for the frightful crimes we have committed against Europe and the whole world."

How Adolf Hitler personally felt about the Germans who followed, believed in and fought for him was revealed during his last hours in a bunker of Berlin, with the Russian Red Army closing in from all sides. Told that the Russians were advancing through a subway tunnel, he commanded, "Flood the tunnel." His generals protested that the subway was being used as a hospital for many wounded German soldiers, who would be drowned.

"So much the worse for them," Hitler snapped.

On the night of April 29, 1945, just before Berlin fell and brought his "Thousand-Year Reich" crashing down in ruins, Hitler shot himself to escape capture and trial for the ghastly crimes of his police state.

7

There are lessons to be learned in why and how Hitler had been able to transform a democracy into a dictatorship.

First, the Weimar Republic failed to do anything to alleviate the severe unemployment in Germany during the Depression. Workers lost faith in the government and trade unions, turning in desperation to the Communists and Nazis.

Then the parties of the Center and Left failed to unite against an obvious menace from the extreme Right. They fought among themselves for political advantage instead. Although the Nazis represented only 37% of the popular vote in July 1932, the disunity of the anti-Nazi majority gave Hitler and his followers the opportunity to rise to power unimpeded.

Meanwhile the Reichstag, torn by quarrels, increasingly permitted President Hindenburg to rule by decree, ignoring the legislature that expressed the people's will. This fatal weakening of the Weimar constitution made it possible for Hitler to win his power through Hindenburg, then exercise that power free of restraints by the Reichstag. Rule by leader replaced the Weimar Republic's principle of rule by democratic law.

Three years before Hitler came to power, Chancellor Joseph Wirth told the Reichstag, "Parliamentarianism is not sick because it is threatened by dictators; it is threatened by dictators because Parliament has abdicated." Thus, after he became Chancellor, Hitler was allowed by a paralyzed Reichstag to pass his Enabling Act, undermining the constitution by giving him dictatorial powers for at least four years.

The failure of German intellectuals to take Hitler seriously was also a mistake. "We made fun of his poor German, his bombastic style," related German playwright Carl Zuckmayer, "and were convinced that such a half-educated fool could never be taken seriously in Germany, a nation of scholars and professors, let alone have the faintest chance of achieving leadership. Millions of leaderless Germans did take him seriously; they heard him speak a language they understood. . . . Not educated to think politically and not willing to learn how, a great many Germans succumbed to quackery and tyranny."

(We might speculate on how many Americans today think politically, or are willing to learn how.)

A hysterical fear of Communism, deliberately engendered by the German Right and the Nazis, also played into Hitler's hands. Millions of lower-middle-class Germans, frightened by the specter of a "Bolshevik takeover," blindly supported the Nazis in violent, unconstitutional attacks on the Left that led eventually to the establishment of the Fascist police state.

They permitted Hitler to get away with the outrageous fraud of the Reichstag fire, by which he inspired anti-Communist panic just before the elections that won the Nazis 288 seats.

"Many people saw in Hitler's movement the best, and probably the only, defense," explained Franz von Papen.

Once people become mobs, the worst human instincts are easily inflamed—greed, fear, hatred, prejudice. A skillful demagogue like Hitler exploited the lowest impulses of the German people, playing upon their emotions like the keys of a mighty organ, as he orchestrated a symphony of terror.

The spiritual leaders of the German people were not blameless. Pastor Martin Niemoeller, who eventually opposed Hitler heroically and went to a concentration camp, later admitted ruefully that he had stood aside when the Nazis attacked the Communists, because he was not a Communist. He had done nothing when they attacked the Socialists because he was not a Socialist. He had still done nothing when the Nazis attacked the schools, the press and the Jews. When they attacked the church, he finally led a protest, because he was a churchman. But by that time it was too late. The point: Liberty is indivisible. If someone else's freedom can be taken away, so can yours.

In *Mein Kampf* Hitler had written frankly, "The right to personal freedom comes second in importance to the duty of maintaining the race." Germans who followed him knew that he planned to abolish individual freedom and demand strict obedience to the arbitrary dictates of a police state. Many, used to authoritarianism except for the dozen or so years of the Weimar Republic, were relieved to be free of the care of decision making, and were willing to submit to the orders of a strong leader who promised to give meaning to their empty lives. Surrendering to Hitler's mystique, they were content to goosestep in rhythm, enjoying the thunder of Germany's march to a world "greatness" they could share. Glorifying him as a national messiah, they followed him blindly.

The Third Reich demonstrated the fatal fascination of Fascist symbols and rituals for unthinking millions—the hypnotic effects of a sea of flags and banners, military parades, impressive uniforms, regimented spectacles. People who feel small are often eager to become part of something big and impressive, compensating for their sense of powerlessness.

The Nazis were also helped to power by cynical Germans who knew Hitler to be either a raving fanatic or mad, yet who saw in his bandwagon an opportunity for personal advantage. Becoming his bureaucrats, they carried out with cynical expertise the crimes he ordered, confident that Nazi power would make it unlikely that they would ever be tried as criminals.

The generals of Nazi Germany, who made common cause with Hitler and his gangsters, dignified Nazi atrocities by swearing loyalty to Hitler. Despising him personally, they nevertheless cooperated with him in order to rearm and regain the military glory they had lost in World War I. When they finally realized their mistake and sought to remove him by assassination, it was too late. They plunged over the precipice with him.

"No nation, when selecting its leader, can foresee what characteristics in him will eventually gain the upper hand," declared Admiral Karl Doenitz in 1958. "And the lesson to be learned from that is that any constitution must be framed so that it is able to prevent the misuse of power by the individual, and that it must be based on the principle of freedom and justice for the community as a whole."

He added, "Every decent German today is ashamed of the crimes which the Third Reich committed behind the nation's back." Still, he insisted that these crimes were the work of a "small minority," without the knowledge of most Germans. Against this view must be set the fact that after the war it was almost impossible to find *any* German willing to admit that he had known what was going on. *What* concentration camps? *What* torture? *What* mass executions?

Noted correspondent Martha Gellhorn wrote in April 1945, "No one is a Nazi. No one ever was. . . . One asks oneself how the detested Nazi government, to which no one paid allegiance, managed to carry on this war for five and a half years. Obviously, not a man, woman or child in Germany ever approved of the war for a minute, according to them."

The unhappy truth was that many millions of Germans were guilty of actively supporting a police state whose dictator had told them in advance that he intended to destroy freedom and democracy, and conquer the world.

"A thousand years will pass," acknowledged Hans Frank, the Nazi Governor General of Poland before he was hanged at Nuremberg in October 1946 for war crimes, "and the guilt of Germany will not be erased."

III

Police State, Russian Style

The Russia of Tsar Nicholas was a grim place to live in the early part of the 20th century. The life of peasants was so harsh that few lived past the age of thirty. In the cities workers were ruthlessly exploited, and thrown out of jobs as the introduction of machinery let more and more women and children take their places in mills and factories at starvation wages under miserable conditions. A month's work, thirteen hours a day, was needed to buy a pair of boots. Hunger, suffering and brutal treatment were the lot of the Russian masses.

Hatred for the Russian ruling class was widespread. An attempt at revolution in 1905 failed, and was bloodily punished by the Tsar's cossack army. Terrorists struck back, assassinating over 200 Tsarist officials. Intellectuals as well as radicals were spied on, arrested and banished to freezing Siberia by Russian secret police, the Okhrana. Many fled to Europe to build new revolutionary movements in exile.

Russian unrest soared when the Tsar took the nation into World War I against Germany. The Russians had no stomach for dying for the Tsar in badly led battles against the powerful German army. In 2 years they suffered 7 million casualties, including almost 3 million dead. Another million ragged soldiers deserted, returning home to join the growing ranks of peasants who were demanding ownership of land. **1981242**

Almost half a million workers in the nation's capital went out on strike to protest the war and growing famine. Many troops joined them. In the countryside deserting soldiers seized land and threatened to burn down the homes of big landowners. The Tsar found himself helpless when his troops refused to put down the disorders. On March 15, 1917, he was forced to abdicate in favor of a Provisional Government composed of middle-class deputies of his parliament, the Duma. Years earlier, the Tsar had consented to creation of the Duma in the vain hope that this concession would quiet revolutionary unrest.

The Social Revolutionary party, a moderate Duma faction representing the peasantry, elected Aleksandr Kerenski to head the new government. Kerenski sought to continue the unpopular war while at the same time pacifying the discontented masses. But he was powerless to satisfy either the workers' demands for higher wages or the peasants' demands for land.

His authority was challenged by a Soviet (Council) of Workers' and Soldiers' Deputies that met separately in Petrograd, the capital. Communist militants of the Bolshevik party grew increasingly influential in this Soviet and in those that sprang up in other Russian cities.

When antiwar agitation threatened to topple Kerenski's government, in desperation he ordered troops to disperse the rioting crowds by firing upon them. He also ordered the arrest of two brilliant Bolshevik leaders—Nikolai Lenin, who escaped to Finland, and Leon Trotsky, who was jailed.

The Russian army suffered disastrous military reverses at the front. Blaming the incompetent Kerenski government, Army Commander-in-Chief Lavr Kornilov led troops against Petrograd to topple the regime. Kerenski appealed to sailors of the nearby Kronstadt naval base to "save the Revolution."

He agreed to their condition—the release of Trotsky. Freed, the Bolshevik leader organized a defense force of sailors, soldiers and civilians into a new Red Guard army. Kornilov was stopped.

Although the Bolsheviks were only a small party, they won increasing popularity by raising dramatic slogans to appeal to the Russian masses. An end to the disastrous war! Bread for all! Land for the peasants! Confiscation of profits! All power to the Soviets!

Peasant delegates joined the Petrograd Soviet, which now claimed the right to issue decrees in defiance of the Kerenski government. Because their party was so small, Bolshevik leaders felt required to agree to participate in Russia's first election, scheduled for November 25, 1917, to choose a new democratic government. They were sharply criticized for this by Lenin, who had returned to Russia to lead the Bolshevik party.

"We don't want a bourgeois democracy," he said flatly. "We don't want any government except the Soviet of workers, soldiers, and poor peasants' deputies!"

The delegates of the Petrograd Soviet chose the popular Trotsky president of the Soviet. A human dynamo, he sped around Petrograd's factories and barracks rallying workers and soldiers behind the revolutionary forces. Meanwhile the Bolsheviks held secret meetings to plot the overthrow of Kerenski's government.

If Lenin was the brains and driving force behind the Russian Revolution, Trotsky was its spokesman and military leader. A shrewd tactician, he conceived of a plan which would let the insurrectionists take power without civil war.

In the dark early morning hours of October 25, as Petrograd slept, he sent armed Red Guard units and insurgent soldiers fanning silently through the city. They occupied all points of control—the state bank, the electric works, the post office, the railroad station, the telephone exchange, the power stations. Other revolutionary forces surrounded the Winter Palace housing the Provisional Government.

When the citizens of Petrograd awoke, Russia's capital had fallen into the Soviet's hands without a shot. That night Kerenski fled, and the ministers of the Provisional Government surrendered. A Council of People's Commissars, all of its members Bolsheviks, took power.

2

Lenin was named Chairman of the new government. Trotsky became Minister of Foreign Affairs, entrusted with the task of getting Russia out of the world war by engineering a treaty with the Germans. Lenin tried but failed to postpone the elections for a new democratic assembly that the Petrograd Soviet had scheduled prior to the Revolution. The Social Revolutionary party, with strong ties to the peasantry, won 58% of the vote. The Bolsheviks won only 29%.

Lenin and Trotsky decided to sabotage the new democratic constituent assembly so that it never functioned. When that parliament met at Petrograd's Tauride Palace in January 1918, Bolshevik troops suddenly seized the palace, turned out the lights and declared the Assembly dissolved.

Lenin and Trotsky controlled Russia as an "Executive Committee." A special organization of secret police, called the Cheka, was set up to deal with opponents of Bolshevik rule.

For seven years until his death, Lenin led a seven-man government called the Politburo, which ruled without challenge. As supreme leader of a Russia renamed the Union of Soviet Socialist Republics (USSR or Soviet Union), Lenin's recommendations invariably prevailed in the Politburo.

His "Decree for Peace," announcing Russia's determination to withdraw from the war, won great support for the Bolshevik (now renamed Communist) dictatorship. This was followed by another popular decree nationalizing land owned by the Tsar, church, monasteries and wealthy landlords. It gave legal sanction to the seizure of estates by peasants all over Russia.

A practical revolutionary, Lenin was shrewd enough to perceive that even if he had the support of every man in the country, he would still have only 50% of the people behind his efforts to tear down the tradition-bound, male-dominated structure of old Russian society. He pressed for the liberation of Russian women as a powerful source of energy to sweep away the old order and usher in the new.

But Russian defenders of male privilege did not surrender easily. In Turkmenia, a Moslem province, a new school for Soviet women resulted in the murder of a wife by her husband in broad daylight. She had dared attend against his orders.

"While here she spoke to men, thus losing respect," he explained to the Moslem judge. "It was my duty to kill her."

But of course, agreed the judge, and set him free.

In Bukhara a woman was arrested and jailed for speaking to a man on the street, even though she was president of the women's branch of the local Communist party. In Uzbekistan an educated citizen refused to teach his wife to read and write.

"What for?" he demanded. "A donkey can't learn anything."

38

When it was pointed out that a woman had a head on her shoulders, he shrugged. "So what? Dogs do, too!"

Lenin's next decree freed Soviet women from the religious and legal bonds that had chained them throughout Russian history. They were declared the equals of men, with equal rights. The church was dispensed with as a sanctifier of marriage. Now, to be legal, vows had to be taken before a government clerk. Divorce was automatically granted to either party of a marriage requesting it. Children born out of wedlock were given rights equal to those of children born to married couples. Married women were given the right to keep their maiden names.

This reversal of male supremacy—strikingly different from the attitude of later Fascist states—understandably created an uproar, especially in rural areas. Critics accused Lenin of seeking to destroy Russian morality and the Russian family. Some charged him with trying to put the country into the hands of "illiterate household cooks."

He tried to explain: "Our aim is to involve more and more women in the task of running the country. . . . Elect women workers! . . . We know that cooks cannot start running the country. . . . But we demand that the task of running the country be taught immediately to every household cook. . . . Ruling the country, woman will learn quickly, and will catch up with man. . . . There are more constructive talents among working and peasant women than we suspect."

Lenin tried to make the people believe that his Communist government was chosen on a basis of "democratic centralism." According to this concept, Communist party members elected delegates to local conferences. The conferences elected delegates to the next highest governing body. It in turn elected delegates to a National Party Congress. The Congress elected a Central Committee. It in turn elected the Politburo and a Secretariat to carry out the daily work of the party.

In actual practice, this power pyramid operated in reverse, from the top down. The Politburo preselected the slate of delegates to be elected to the Central Committee. It preselected the slate to be elected to the National Party Congress, and so on down the line. The result was a concentration of dictatorial power in Lenin's hands. All other governmental bodies served primarily to rubber-stamp his decisions, and to see to it that his orders were carried out.

According to Lenin, the Soviet Union now had a "dictatorship of the proletariat," or working classes, which represented a beginning "Socialist phase" of the Communist revolution. It was intended to transform Russia's capitalist economy into one wholly owned and operated by the people themselves. Until this could be done, however, some inequality would continue to prevail. Under Socialism people would have to be rewarded unequally, according to ability and merit, to encourage all to do their best.

Lenin promised that later, when there was no further need for dictatorship, the government would "wither away" into a pure Communist state. Then everyone would share the wealth of the nation without regard to inequality of ability, in some undefined manner—"each according to his need."

Democracy would be less than "truly complete" under Socialism, Lenin admitted. But he explained that the proletariat, in whose name he ostensibly ruled, needed to be led and could not be trusted to determine policy by itself. Nevertheless, he insisted, "the Soviet government is a million times more democratic than the most democratic bourgeois republic."

Moving the capital from Petrograd to Moscow, Lenin declared, "We, the Bolsheviks, have convinced Russia and we have conquered her. Now we must govern her." To Lenin that meant *total control* of all institutions and organizations, from every government structure to industry, farms, labor unions, schools and the press. It also meant complete suppression of all opposition to his policies; opposition was branded "counterrevolutionary" and therefore punishable. The law of the land was what the Communist party, making up less than 1% of the population, said it was. No twisting of words could disguise the fact that the dictatorship was *over* the proletariat, not of it.

This did not mean that Lenin, Trotsky and the Communist party were not popular or admired. Indeed, many of the people felt that their leadership represented the best hope for a better life. President Wilson sent diplomat William C. Bullitt, who later became intensely anti-Soviet, and journalist Lincoln Steffens on a secret mission to the Soviet Union. They reported finding most of the people enthusiastic about the Bolsheviks, despite widespread famine and disease aggravated by civil war and a blockade of Soviet ports.

Actual Communist party membership was deliberately kept small by Lenin, who believed in a revolutionary elite of dedicated, tightly disciplined Marxists, rather than in a sprawling, factionalized mass party.

3

Lenin's chief opposition came from the antigovernment Anarchists and the peasant-oriented Revolutionary Socialists who made several attempts on his life. They were fought as counterrevolutionaries by the Cheka, and enormous numbers were despatched by firing squads.

The Cheka, the Soviet secret police force, has been reorganized over the years in many different guises—GPU, OGPU, NKVD, NKGB, SMERSH, MGB and KGB, its present designation. Its chief function has always remained the same—working in secret to suppress opposition to the Communist regime in power. The place for opposition parties, Lenin made no bones about saying, "is in prison."

In 1921, civil war was waged against the Communist regime by rebellious White Russian ethnic armies backed by the Western powers, who sent armies to intervene in Siberia. The Cheka instituted a reign of terror against all real and suspected enemies of the regime. Their homes were broken into and searched; they were seized, imprisoned, tortured and executed without trial. "The Cheka's aim," explained a Cheka official, "is that the mere mention of its name will make everybody abandon any idea of sabotage, extortion or conspiracy."

Lenin declared, "The Terror was forced upon us when the world powers turned their military forces against us. . . . We should not have held out for two days had we not fought off the attacks of officers and White Guards, and that meant Terror. . . . The use of violence was caused by the need to suppress exploiters, landowners and capitalists. . . . Once this task is completed, we shall relinquish all the special measures."

But Cheka terrorism persisted even after the civil war was won. Prisons overflowed, and forced-labor camps were opened for both convicts and political prisoners. Killing an estimated 50,000 victims, the Cheka inspired fear, bitterness and hatred among the masses. Lenin was forced to tell the 9th Party Congress, "It is necessary to restrict the institution to a purely political sphere. We say emphatically that it is time to reform the Cheka."

The civil war left the country in a shambles. Industry was paralyzed. Transport facilities were wrecked. Towns and cities lay in ruin. Everything was in short supply. Peasants refused to sell food to the cities for Soviet paper money. Communist Red Army troops seized their wheat forcibly, providing a daily bread ration that amounted to less than two ounces a person.

Millions of fugitives clogged the roads, fleeing from famine and epidemics. One ragged refugee lamented, "We have come from one cemetery to fall into another." Hordes of "wild boys of the road," orphaned by catastrophe, roamed the country looting and killing for food. An estimated 5 million Russians died of hunger and its effects.

One embittered labor delegate went to see Lenin to protest the miserable conditions of workers. Inside Lenin's office, he stared at the famous leader's threadbare suit and scuffed, worn, old shoes. Emerging, he told his comrades, "He received me like a brother, but when I saw his shoes I didn't dare ask him for anything!"

Lenin gratefully accepted assistance from the American Relief Administration (ARA), which came to the rescue of starving Soviet women and children. But the Cheka later arrested thousands of Russians who worked for the ARA distributing relief aid. They were charged with "counterrevolutionary activity." There was some evidence that a number of them, indeed, had been recruited in an American network of anti-Soviet spies.

Sailors of the Kronstadt fortress, who had helped bring about the Revolution, became disillusioned with Lenin's regime. Rebelling with cries of "Death to the Bolsheviks!" they were crushed by the Cheka and Red troops. The revolt shook Lenin.

He decided that the only way out of the Soviet Union's economic difficulties was to stimulate production of food and manufactures by temporarily permitting private trade for peasants, small factory owners and shopkeepers. This New Economic Policy (NEP), which lasted seven years, put the Soviet economy back on its feet and gave the Communists a breathing spell. But life remained desperately poor, incredibly hard.

Having liberated women from the home, Lenin enlisted them in his struggle to build a greater Soviet Union. Under a universal labor draft, they joined men in digging ditches, operating heavy machinery, and repairing factories and plants. Many were ordered to remote wilderness areas to build and operate new industrial complexes.

"In our ideals there is no place for the use of force against people," Lenin wrote. Yet, paradoxically, he believed that without the use of force—at least at first—the Communists would not be able to prevent political enemies from wrecking his program to create the conditions needed for democratic Socialism.

"The lives of our children will be better than ours," he promised the Russian people. "Much of what we have lived through will be spared them; their lives will be less cruel. But I do not envy them. Our generation accomplished a task of astounding historical importance. The cruelty of our lives, imposed by circumstances, will be understood and forgiven. Everything will be understood—*everything!*"

4

But Soviet history took an unexpected turn with the death of Lenin in 1924. He had made one serious political blunder. He had appointed Joseph Stalin, a crafty, power-hungry Communist bureaucrat, to the minor post of Party Secretary. Stalin secretly built up the Secretariat until it became his own personal political machine. By the time Lenin realized that Stalin had made himself virtual boss of the Communist party, it was too late. Stalin was so powerful that he was even able to resist Lenin's attempts to expose and remove him.

After 5 years of political maneuvering, Stalin, who had won control of the secret police, was able to purge his rivals ruthlessly by either execution or exile. Leon Trotsky, who had expected to inherit Lenin's mantle as supreme leader, was first exiled, then murdered in Mexico by Stalin's secret police. Stalin maintained his personal dictatorship for 25 years, until his death in 1953. Under him, Lenin and Trotsky's policy of putting the goal of world revolution ahead of narrow national interests was dropped. In its place Stalin mounted an aggressive drive for supremacy of the Soviet Union.

Not a hysterical psychopath like Hitler, Stalin was nevertheless a cold-blooded leader who did not hesitate to massacre millions of people the way a shrewd chess player sacrifices pawns to win a match. The first pawns to feel his merciless power were the kulaks —Russian peasants who owned their own farms.

They had been dismayed when the Revolution had ordered them to give up private ownership of land so that their holdings could be combined into collective farms. They resisted violently. Officials who sought to enforce the decree were attacked and driven off.

Stalin responded by "liquidating" the kulaks—driving them off their lands and out of their homes into exile in a system of forced-labor camps known as GULAG. Millions bitterly destroyed their livestock and farming equipment before these could be seized. Some 10 million paid for this defiance by being slaughtered by Stalin's secret police.

In 1928 Stalin began the first Five-Year Plan to industrialize the Soviet Union at top speed, as Lenin had wanted. Proclaiming it a success, he followed it with successive Five-Year Plans to develop both heavy and light industries.

Although serious mistakes were made, no one dared question Stalin's decisions. The Communist party, Russians were told, was infallible because its judgments were based on "scientifically correct Marxism-Leninism." In practice, that meant Stalin could never be wrong, since it was he who made all decisions for the party. All party bureaus, governing bodies and courts of law possessed the power to do exactly what Stalin wanted—no more and no less.

He grew increasingly paranoiac. Stalin was positive that plots were being hatched against him on every hand, perhaps because of his guilty conscience over the millions of people he had had killed. During the years 1935–1939 he ordered mass purges of the Communist party, resorting to police terror on a grand scale. Officials suspected of opposing Stalin were arrested and tortured into confessing at public trials to acts of treason. Moscow even furnished local police with a percentage quota of the number of local citizens to be arrested.

Stalin did not bother with trials for hundreds of thousands of rank-and-file party members, who were simply shot, exiled or shipped to GULAG camps along with party leaders.

Former U.S. Supreme Court Justice William O. Douglas investigated the Soviet method of persecuting political prisoners. "The prisoner seldom appeared before the court," he reported. "No counsel represented him. He had no notice of the charge or even of the trial. He merely received notice that he had been convicted. The charges were often fancied or manufactured. The sentences usually ran for five years; and if at the end of that time the prisoner was still alive, another judgment would be entered—again *in absentia*—extending the sentence for another five years."

GULAG prisoners were virtually starved on 2,400 calories a day —bare subsistence when doing hard labor for long hours. Harsh reprisals, and a reduction to 1,300 calories a day, punished anyone who protested or resisted.

"It is a machine for accelerating death," said one survivor. Estimates of the number of Stalin victims who died in the camps range as high as 20 million during his years in power. A Soviet heart surgeon, Professor N. Amosoff, explained why there was no great outcry from the Russian people:

"Of course we young enthusiasts knew all about those purges, but as long as they hit the party echelons, simple people did not react. The propaganda pressure was so relentless that many felt those people were real enemies of the people, and had to be dealt with in the harshest manner. . . . The [Five-Year] Plan had to be fulfilled no matter how many victims this entailed."

Stalin was not content merely to dispose of his important political victims bodily. He also ordered their names expunged from all Soviet records, rewriting history as though they had never existed. Students growing up under Stalin were taught that the two architects of the Russian Revolution were not Lenin and Trotsky, but Lenin and Stalin.

Stalin proved an able war leader. Under him the Soviet Union survived six years of terrible assault by Nazi Germany during World War II that cost the lives of over 20 million Russians.

When Stalin's armies fought back through eastern Europe on their way to Berlin, many Russian soldiers were stunned by the higher standard of living they found in most countries they liberated. Serving in the army of occupation that forced the countries of eastern Europe to install Communist governments, Soviet troops became "infected" with an admiration for Western ways of life and culture.

When they and prisoners of war returned home, they were regarded suspiciously by Stalin as potential troublemakers. Once again he began accusing thousands of Communists of being foreign agents. Secret police spied on Politburo members, party leaders and other bureaucrats. Stalin also became convinced of a secret plot by Jewish doctors to murder him. He ordered them arrested and beaten into confessions of guilt.

When Stalin suddenly died on March 5, 1953, his police chief, Lavrenti Beria, declared, "Now it will be quiet for a little while—and then there will come a new wave of terror." But a group of Politburo leaders who had long suffered under Stalin were determined to reform the system.

While Stalin's dictatorship had been an unmitigated reign of terror, he had nevertheless consolidated the Revolution and made impressive economic gains for the Soviet economy. He had done it by inspiring enthusiasm primarily among young workers without proper tools, at least half of them girls who had never used a tool before, under conditions of severe hardship and poverty.

"No other nation in the world could afford to pay so horrible a price for its industrial revolution as Russia did," observed one-time President of Czechoslovakia Eduard Benes. "That's what makes Russia so different from other nations. The very endurance of her people baffles the Westerner. It is both monstrous and stupendous."

"Those were magnificent years," recalled heart surgeon Dr. N. Amosoff, "when we saw industrial plants and schools rising all around us, and we felt that there was no limit to our dreams. And there was no sacrifice we were not willing to make to see those dreams come true."

Stalin made primary education compulsory, with over half the students being girls. By 1935 he had wiped out illiteracy in every Russian under 35 years of age. For their impressive educational and industrial advances, however, the Russian people had been forced to submit to rule by a police state with an entrenched machinery of terror.

5

Stalin was replaced by enthusiastic, aggressive Nikita Khrushchev, who had suffered under Stalin's arrogant rule and was aware of widespread discontent over the suppression of dissent. In 1956 he shocked and astonished the Communist world, which had been led by Kremlin propagandists to view Stalin as a kindly, noble-minded, farsighted Soviet leader.

Khrushchev accused him of "mass arrests and deportations of thousands of people, execution without trial and without normal investigation . . . barbaric tortures . . . lying, slanderous and absurd accusations." Stalin had developed a "personality cult," Khrushchev charged, to glorify himself and concentrate all power into his own hands alone.

Khrushchev's denunciation broke the silence that had smothered the crimes of the late tyrant. Hopes for political freedom soared as dissidents in the Communist puppet states of Eastern Europe, as well as in the Soviet Union, were allowed to speak out against Stalin's concealed atrocities. The de-Stalinization movement ushered in a period of political relaxation. Communist intellectuals pressed for greater liberty of press and speech.

Khrushchev drastically curtailed the powers of the secret police. Releasing some political prisoners, he improved conditions in the GULAG camps. Laws were tightened to make only acts specifically forbidden by the penal code punishable as crimes. Judges were instructed to rule only on evidence, not on mere suspicion of guilt. At the Communist Party Congress in early 1959 the people were told, "Revolutionary legality has been fully restored, and those guilty of its violations punished."

The new Soviet leader sought to introduce a new era of harmony and goodwill both at home and abroad. Farmers, workers and consumers were appeased by concessions to improve the quality of Soviet life. At the same time Khrushchev reversed Stalin's postwar policy of hostility toward the United States, seeking to end the "Cold War" between the two countries. He offered the Americans "peaceful coexistence."

Under the new policy each country would benefit from Soviet-American trade, scientific and cultural relations, and money-saving disarmament treaties. This "détente," reducing the threat of nuclear war, was later agreed to in 1972 by President Nixon.

Khrushchev incurred important enemies within the Soviet bureaucracy who owed all their power and privileges to Stalinism, and were not happy with de-Stalinization. The most serious problem for Khrushchev came from the people of the satellite countries of Eastern Europe. Excited and encouraged by his new liberalization policy, they sought to revolt against the puppet rule imposed upon them from Moscow. Unrest spread swiftly, causing an uprising in Hungary, which Khrushchev promptly crushed with Soviet tanks for fear of similar uprisings all through Eastern Europe.

When his political enemies convinced a majority of the Politburo that Khrushchev had committed too many foreign policy blunders, he was deposed as Party Secretary in October 1964. His successor, Leonid Brezhnev, continued to pursue the policy of foreign détente, but cracked down hard on internal dissent. The de-Stalinization movement was brought to a halt. Soviet historians were ordered to prepare a "slightly more balanced" evaluation of Stalin's role in developing the USSR. Intellectuals who persisted in criticizing the government found themselves harassed, arrested and put away in work camps or mental institutions by purge-type trials.

When Czech leaders sought to soften their Communist rule by liberalizing it with a "human face," Brezhnev saw the move as a threat to Moscow's control of all the satellite countries in Eastern Europe. He sent troops into Prague to crush an uprising in support of the Czech government. The liberalization policy was abruptly wiped out.

A bluff, hearty bear of a man, Brezhnev was no cold-blooded tyrant like Stalin. The Soviet Union under his leadership was less oppressive. But it was still a police state, persecuting all who dared to dissent.

Under the dictatorship of the Communists, the Soviet people have come a long way from the miseries they suffered in Tsarist days. All citizens are now guaranteed jobs, housing, medical care and pensions. But they still lack the right to go where they please, say or write what they like publicly, or turn out of office government leaders they don't want.

6

If you had lived in Lenin's police state, you might have been among those oppressed by Tsarism who hailed the drastic changes in Russian society as changes for the better. You might have approved of Stalin, too, because of the country's giant economic strides under his rule. And because either his acts of terror didn't touch you personally or you believed the propaganda that the victims were all guilty of treason.

As an average Soviet citizen you would have welcomed the reforms and liberalization policies of Khrushchev, while perhaps feeling embarrassed by the image of a boorish peasant he projected on the international scene. Under Brezhnev you would have strongly approved continuing the policy of détente, but probably wished that the Soviet Union could move faster toward catching up with the American standard of living.

As a Soviet citizen today, you would find both benefits and problems under the Soviet police state. Technically, education would be free for you from first grade to the university. But you would have less than a 10% chance of winning the competition for a place in a university or other higher educational institute. The government regulates education to provide more factory workers and field hands, fewer executives and professionals.

Consequently, at the end of 8 years of primary school you would be required to begin productive work. At the same time you would be encouraged to go on with your studies through evening schools or correspondence courses. At the end of a three-year period you would get a secondary-school certificate which would give you a shot at higher education. Provided you had the proper political influence —recommendations by the Party, your trade union, the Komsomol (Communist youth organization) and the director of your work program.

In effect, if you were critical of government policies and rash enough to indicate it, you would never get the university training necessary for the best jobs. Furthermore, the bureaucracy makes certain that children of upper-bracket families get placed in light work, which gives them an advantage in studying and competing for university admission.

The reality for most Soviet youth is immediate compulsory labor in the workshops or fields after the eighth year of school. The primary concern of the government is not your development along the lines of your ambition or talents, but the training of masses of youths in the technical skills needed to keep Soviet farms and factories operating. Understandably, many young people resent forced physical labor, especially at so early a stage in life. Those who resist, and seek to study independently instead while supported by their parents, are subject to up to five years of compulsory labor for "abstaining from socially useful work and living an antisocial and parasitic life."

Even those who get to the university are expected to help with summer harvests, for token pay. Upon graduation they also have to spend two to three years working wherever the state decides that their services are needed. Often this is a remote rural area in need of trained personnel because few Soviet citizens voluntarily choose to live there.

Many students get to an institute of higher education for a year or two, and emerge with the title of "engineer." Often, however, they are little more than slightly qualified supervisors trained to do relatively simple jobs.

As a student you would not be allowed to think objectively. Your history textbook would teach you, for example, that the Soviet Union had already defeated Nazi Germany in World War II by the time the Americans landed in Normandy. That it was the Soviet entry into the war against Japan that compelled Tokyo to surrender, not the American use of atomic weapons.

A 1971 poll indicated that only half of Russian high-school students sampled even knew that the United States had fought in World War II. Another 25% thought we had fought on the Nazi side.

In Stalin's writings on history and politics, he frequently lied or distorted facts, to which he added the persuasive phrase, "as is known." Since Stalin asserted that these were established facts, what Russian scholar would be daring or foolhardy enough to demand proof?

Soviet history textbooks, too, are full of patriotic "revelations." Did you know that a Russian navy instructor named Aleksandr Popov discovered and demonstrated radio a year before Marconi? That a Russian professor named Boris Rozing invented TV in 1907? That a Russian captain built the world's first airplane in 1882? If you doubt these claims, obviously it is because you are "a victim of capitalist brainwashing."

"Under state absolutism," noted Bertram D. Wolfe in his book *Communist Totalitarianism*, "history, as all of culture, has been 'nationalized' and there are no individual viewpoints or private judgments."

Until 1965 you might also have run into trouble if you were working in agriculture and trying to improve grains by interbreeding the best strains. The reason: In 1948 Stalin endorsed the ideas of Trofim D. Lysenko, an agronomist with no scientific training who insisted that plant traits could be changed simply by changing their environment. Scientists who protested were denounced as "enemies of the progress of Soviet science and the Soviet people." Accordingly, Soviet agriculture was seriously set back for 17 years.

As a Soviet citizen you would have access to free medical services, wherever you lived. You would have to pay for only a few medicines. The chances are that your doctor would be a woman. There are more doctors for the population than we have, all extremely well trained. One major drawback: You could not select your own doctor. But your life expectancy would now be 70 years, compared to only 44 during the first decade of Soviet rule.

The regimented society does not, nevertheless, escape many of the ills that beset capitalist societies—alcoholism, drug addiction, vandalism, juvenile delinquency and street crime. So many Russians get drunk on payday that worried Soviet authorities are trying to change the pay system by depositing salaries in savings banks. A wry Russian joke runs, "What is alcoholism? Answer: an intermediate stage between Socialism and Communism."

7

You would not only have a right to a job, but also the *obligation* to work if you are able. "He who does not work," says the Soviet Constitution, "does not eat." You would have to carry and be prepared to show official work papers on demand, if you were a man or unmarried woman. Otherwise you might be exiled as a "parasite" on Soviet society.

Unless your particular skill was in great demand in a city where you wished to live, you would have to work where the state needed you. You could not move legally from the countryside to a city in search of a job. Nor could you go out on strike, or have a union bargain to get you better terms.

You would be subject to pressure from fellow workers not to be an absentee, except in case of serious illness. Bureaucrats directing the enterprise would seek to encourage you to increase your output on the job. Not by offering more money, but by pinning your photo to a factory "Board of Honor."

As a factory worker, your life would be regimented around the factory and its benefits. Ostensibly, your trade union would represent and protect your interests. In reality, it would work hand in glove with management to extract the greatest productivity out of you and your fellow workers. It would tolerate dangerous working conditions, speed up assembly lines, and suppress any expression of serious dissatisfaction.

On the other hand, your children would enjoy factory parks, playground equipment, nurseries and day-care centers. The factory union would send them to summer camp, and offer you a rest camp for your own vacation. You could buy a good meal inexpensively at the factory lunchroom. The factory would also try to keep you contented by providing cultural entertainment, library services, and opportunities to learn and practice the arts.

You would receive similar benefits if you worked on a collective or state farm. On a collective, which is essentially a village, you would live in a community with shops, schools, a library, a hospital and theaters. You would share in the profits—or losses. Your collective would be required to produce and deliver to the state a large percentage of its produce—at prices set by the state. You would also be permitted to work your own private plot of land in your spare time, and sell what you raised independently.

If you worked on a state farm, which is essentially an agricultural factory, you would be paid a guaranteed salary regardless of the harvest. Here, too, you could also operate your own small garden enterprise on the side.

Your pay would be on the basis of "each according to his ability" —or, in practice, usefulness to the state—with a wide range between the lowest and highest salaries. Party officials, government administrators, scientists, writers and other professionals earn far more than factory workers. In general, your standard of living would be about half that of an American in a comparable job. But you would be better off than some 20 million Americans struggling to survive at the poverty level.

Making a mistake on your job could cost you more than just the job. When a woman agronomist, A. G. Skolenko, planted 500 acres with corn so badly that the field had to be resown, she was convicted of criminal negligence and sentenced to one year of "corrective labor"—hard labor at a prison camp.

As an agricultural worker on a collective farm, you would earn less than a factory worker. Like him, you would have little to say about where you were put to work. But your food would be cheaper. And you could sell, in private farm markets, surplus food you grew on your own private plot. That is no small advantage, because food purchases take over half the monthly salaries of most Russians.

One consolation—as a Soviet citizen you would have to pay only a minimal income tax. The government relies upon direct personal taxation for less than 8% of its income, compared to 52% in the American budget. Government operating expenses are derived mainly from indirect taxation—the high prices charged by most state-owned enterprises.

Most prices, except in authorized private markets, are fixed by the government. As a result, the black market thrives in regions where there are shortages. In 1976 the government arrested a ring of Moscow store clerks for secretly selling merchandise to black marketteers, who resold it at a 100% profit in distant provinces. If you bought a used car, for which prices are also fixed, the seller might "walk around the block" with you to demand extra payment for "immediate delivery." Otherwise, how about some time next year?

8

The old inferior position of women in Russian society was abolished by the Soviet Constitution, which declares, "Women in the USSR have equal rights with men . . . with guaranteed employment on an equal basis . . . equal pay for equal work, and equal rest, social security and educational opportunities."

As a woman in the Soviet Union, your opportunities for a professional career would be far greater than in the United States. Women constitute only 4% of American lawyers, but over 35% of Soviet lawyers. In the USSR over 30% of graduate engineers are women, compared to 1/2% in the United States. Over 31% of members elected to the Supreme Soviet are women, compared to only 2% of the members of the American Congress.

But the greatest number of Soviet women—twice as many as men —are employed as unskilled factory and field labor. At an agricultural conference Khrushchev once noted wryly, "It turns out that it is the men who do the administering and the women who do the work." Although women hold half the jobs, they receive only two fifths of the national income.

Your complaint as a working wife and mother would not be very different from that of an American counterpart. Elena Andreyeva, a Soviet writer, pointed out, "Legal equality has not as yet become actual because, in many families, woman continues to carry the entire burden of the housework, in addition to her professional occupation." A 1970 study showed that the average working woman had only half as much time as a man for social activities, reading, adult education and rest. And an hour less sleep at night.

The Soviet government has organized a propaganda campaign to persuade husbands to share housework, shopping and child care with working wives. It is having some impact among the younger, better-educated married men.

Because the Soviet Union is made up of a collection of different nationalities, half the population is non-Russian. If you were one of an ethnic minority group like Estonians, Latvians, Lithuanians, Ukrainians, Georgians or Armenians, you would find that no matter how high you climbed in a job, there would always be ethnic Russians over you. The Russians suspect, not without reason, that many of the nationalities hate the regime, desiring independence under their own ethnic leaders.

From early childhood you would be subjected to propaganda playing down your ethnic origins, emphasizing your obligations as a Soviet citizen and reminding you how extremely lucky you were to be sheltered under the umbrella of the Revolution.

If you were Jewish, and wished to leave the country for Israel or the United States, emigration would be made as difficult for you as possible. You would be charged a heavy exit tax to repay the government for the cost of your education. Many Jews organized protests and hunger strikes, and appealed to Jewish groups in the United States for support. Russian police hauled many off to jail. But intense pressure from Western legislators and universities that threatened to break off academic contacts with the Soviets forced Moscow to let large numbers of Jews emigrate.

Vitaly Rubin, a distinguished Jewish scholar, and his wife were typical victims of police-state tactics. Applying to emigrate to Israel, they had been denied permission on grounds that Rubin was "too valuable to the state to lose." This excuse was exposed as a pretext when he lost his job and could find work only as a laborer. The KGB, the secret police, kept the Rubins under nerve-wracking surveillance, and imprisoned him for eight days during the Nixon visit to Moscow in 1974.

After four and a half years American pressure finally won the Rubins an exit visa. When they sought to mail 108 boxes of Rubin's personal library, officials objected that the stamps with Lenin's picture had been unintentionally pasted upside down, and they were forced to buy new stamps to cover them. Customs officials haggled with them over emigration documents and their furniture right up to the last moment of departure. Vitaly Rubin had to surrender his Jewish Star of David because it was "undeclared gold."

That same month (June 1976) Chicago-born Abe Stolar, his Russian-born wife Gitta and their 17-year-old son Mikhail appealed to world opinion to help them leave the USSR for Israel. Stolar's exit visa was cruelly revoked just as he was about to board a plane. Cancellation of their visas after they had sold their Moscow apartment and shipped all their belongings to Israel left them destitute and homeless, living on the charity of friends. "We are now without clothing or belongings and without any possibility of earning a living," Stolar wrote in a statement given to Western newsmen.

If you were religious, you would be permitted to worship as you pleased, but in school you would be taught that religion is evil; that atheism is the only intelligent belief. You could not be a Communist party member, or stand for public office, if you belonged to a church. Many old churches have been allowed to fall into ruin. Some have been turned into theaters, warehouses and antireligious museums. Nevertheless, on holy days such as Easter, many big city churches are packed with worshippers, particularly the elderly.

9

You could not easily obtain uncensored foreign newspapers to learn what's going on in Russia and in the world. Only a few Moscow newsstands carry American, British or French papers. When the French Communist paper, *L'Humanité*, carried criticism of the Soviet regime, that edition could not be bought anywhere.

As for the Soviet press, you would not read in it any unfavorable news of the USSR, nor of any Communist country except China, with whom the USSR still feuds.

Soviet reporters regard themselves less as newsmen than as "educators" entrusted by the government with "the organization of public opinion," as *Izvestia* newsman Melor G. Sturua put it. Ignoring or minimizing deficiencies and weaknesses in the Soviet system, they help keep the USSR a closed society. Soviet accidents, floods or earthquakes are mentioned only briefly, usually long after they took place, and only in terms of how well they were handled.

You would be fed daily accounts of the worst aspects of Western life—the corruption, murders, scandals, inflation, etc., freely reported by Western media. How dreadful, you might shudder, life must be under a capitalist system!

Censors would make sure you did not see copies of American magazines, less out of fear that you might read the contents than that you might be astonished by the ads featuring cars, color TV sets, microwave ovens, washer-drier units and other luxuries most American workers enjoy.

No famous Russian person who is in the censor bureau's "black book" can be mentioned favorably. To find out what was really going on you would have to read illegal underground newspapers. Such papers, called *samizdat*, are usually typed on thin paper with a maximum number of carbon copies. Passed from hand to hand, they spread censored news about political arrests, trials and sentences. If you had a tape recorder, you would also be able to listen to forbidden songs and poems of protest on cassettes, called *magnitizats*, which are swapped around among dissenters.

All of which could land you in prison under a law prohibiting "agitation or propaganda carried on for the purpose of subverting or weakening Soviet authority or of committing particular, especially dangerous crimes against the State."

An estimated 50,000 secret police prevent dissenters from organizing effective opposition to the government, and all parties except the Communist party remain outlawed, making meaningful change unlikely.

You would find little support for dissenters among the Soviet people, who are conditioned to regard them in much the same way as Americans regard Communists in their midst. Most Soviet citizens are apathetic and indifferent about political trials. Soviet dissenters are forced to look to public opinion abroad as their chief hope of pressuring the government to be less repressive.

Your lack of freedom to speak out against the Soviet system might not bother you greatly. From childhood, after all, you would have been indoctrinated with the belief that only the Communist party can represent all classes in Russia fairly and intelligently. The Western concept of "freedom," you would have been taught, really represents a state of national disorder and lack of government planning. Chaos.

Besides, didn't the Soviet Constitution guarantee freedom of the press, speech and assembly? And even the facilities by which workers could make their views public? Of course, Soviet authorities made it clear that these freedoms must be exercised "within the discipline of the Communist party." You were permitted to grumble locally about grievances, provided your criticism was not seen as an attack on the party. If it *was*, however, you could find yourself on trial for "slanderous fabrications against the Soviet system and government."

The people in your apartment block or factory would make your behavior and attitudes their business, under direction of the government. Neighborhood and work groups are expected to take responsibility for individual conduct. Pressure would be applied on you to conform to what the government expects of a good citizen. In effect, gossip becomes another way of controlling political dissent. Your best bet for advancement in Soviet society would be to parrot the government line in all things, and even to bear false witness against someone, if you are asked to by a government agent.

"A Communist must be prepared to make every sacrifice," Lenin wrote, "and, if necessary, even resort to all sorts of schemes and stratagems, employ illegitimate methods, conceal the truth."

If you were a Russian dissident trying to make your complaint against the government heard in the outside world, your mail would be censored. Any foreign call you made would be monitored. Newly arrived foreign correspondents would be warned sharply against talking to "doubtful persons" like yourself. Your street conversations would be monitored from 100 feet or more away by the use of small electronic eavesdropping devices.

International fame is no protection for the defiant. Zhordes Medvedev, a world-renowned biochemist, argued publicly that the refusal of Soviet authorities to let Russian scientists travel abroad for extended research was crippling the development of Soviet science and keeping it behind the West. In the spring of 1971 he was confined to a mental hospital. He was only one of many celebrated dissenters punished in this manner.

If you tried to meet with foreign friends, or have dinner with them at their apartments in the international compound, you would probably be arrested and interrogated for hours on the nature of your contacts with them. You would fear to invite foreign friends to your own home, especially since the lack of privacy is such that neighbors would be likely to report you. If a foreign friend wanted you to meet another Russian you did not know, you might refuse out of fear that the KGB would think you were being recruited as a spy.

You could not read any book which the censor did not consider useful in advancing Soviet views, or which at least did not raise awkward questions about the Soviet system. You would be able to read pre-Soviet Russian classics, but in some cases not without censorship. For example, the new Soviet edition of *The Brothers Karamazov* by Fëdor Dostoevski has been shortened by deletion of most of the religious parts.

To fight boredom you might seek distraction at the theater—in films, ballet, plays, opera, concerts. Soviet films tend to be dull propaganda, but other forms of cultural entertainment are generally of the highest quality.

Many intellectuals in the Soviet Union want greater freedom to write, speak, compose, paint and perform as they please. Not only freedom to express their ideas, but also freedom of style. They have to be careful, however, about provoking the displeasure of the officials who control their jobs. What many of them feel about the police state they live under was expressed by writer Boris Pasternak in his novel *Doctor Zhivago*, published abroad.

Zhivago dreamed of "living on your own land thanks to the toil of your own hands, in complete independence and with no obligation to anyone. But in fact he found that there had merely been a switch from the oppression of the old State to the oppression of the new State, the much harsher yoke of the revolutionary superstate."

Many Russian writers have been arrested for publishing abroad works critical of the Soviet Union. To frighten off spectators at their trials, the KGB snapped photos of all who came to court, and also barred foreign correspondents. The accused writers received six-year sentences in Soviet labor camps. One Russian woman who had typed a "forbidden" manuscript paid for it with a year's imprisonment, and banishment forever from her home city of Moscow. When some Russian intellectuals protested against these trials, they themselves were arrested.

If you stubbornly persisted in opposing such police rule, the KGB would see to it that you lost your job, along with your membership in your union or institute. You could then be exiled to Siberia as a "parasite" on Soviet society, or confined to a mental institution. If the authorities felt you would be less trouble out of the country than in it, you would find yourself banished from the USSR and barred from reentry.

If you were arrested as a dissenter, it would be possible to win acquittal, but your chances would be slim. For one thing, you could be held in jail without counsel or visitors for five months while the prosecutor investigated the charges against you. If during that time you signed a confession—because of coercion, torture or any illegal pressure—that confession would be admissible in court as evidence against you. Sentences tend to be severe.

10

Why, one might ask, aren't the Soviet people thoroughly miserable and longing to revolt, as in Tsarist days? Basically because the kind of life which might be hateful to those used to political and intellectual freedom, to freedom of choice and movement, is not necessarily hateful to those who have been conditioned to control all their lives. Most Soviet citizens and their children today were born under the Red star. They grew up believing that theirs is the best of all possible systems.

Most do not consider themselves suffering under the dictatorship, nor do they think of their government as a police state. According to American journalist John Gunther, they believe that the Soviet Union belongs to *them* as a cooperative enterprise. So they're really working for themselves, aren't they? They don't have to worry about losing their jobs, or being sick or impoverished in their old age, like so many workers and their families in the Western world. (Unless, of course, they fall afoul of the law.) They feel looked after, cared for, safe, secure. Doesn't such a government merit your loyalty and gratitude, comrade? *Especially* from those who enjoy the best opportunities and positions?

Not all dissenters, in fact, want to leave the Soviet Union, any more than all Americans critical of the United States government want to leave *their* country. Before the famous dissenting novelist Aleksandr I. Solzhenitsyn decided to emigrate, he refused to go to Sweden to accept his Nobel Prize in 1970, for fear the Soviet authorities would not allow him to return. A homeland is a precious thing. Dissenters want not exile abroad, but change at home.

The average Soviet citizen is proud of what his country has achieved in the way of industrial development, exploration in space, medicine, science and the building of new cities in what was once vast wasteland. He admires the long way the Communists have brought the country from the primitive world of the Tsar, and is elated by the promise of even more rapid advances in the years ahead. He sees his choices of consumer goods growing steadily, with more and more of life's comforts, including cars and better housing, becoming available.

The average Soviet citizen is also proud that the USSR has, in a relatively short time, become one of the two greatest powers on earth. He is convinced that the rest of the world, sooner or later, will be pressed by the forces of history—as Marx saw it—to turn Communist along Soviet lines.

Perhaps most important of all, young Russians who are the sons and daughters of once-illiterate poor peasants have been permitted to rise to positions of importance. John Gunther noted, "They do not, as young people in America might, think of themselves as 'self-made'; they think of themselves as *state*-made."

Not that Russians do not complain about the all-powerful secret police, collective farming or the clumsy, wasteful bureaucracy. There is dissatisfaction and discontent about these and other Soviet sore points but not—for the vast majority—to the point of resistance or protest. For many it is enough that the blatant terrorism of the Stalin era has been replaced by a police state which, while stern, is considerably less fearsome. Ordinary citizens no longer tremble in fear of a knock on the door in the middle of the night.

As one used to living in a democracy, however, you would find it inconceivable to vote in elections which let you vote only for one set of candidates—Communist party members—and would not even let you write in other names on your ballot. You would be understandably cynical about a government which began by promising everyone equality, yet still has so many favored classes who enjoy higher salaries and special privileges.

Moreover, you might wonder why a government which calls itself Communist is still only "in transition from Socialism to Communism" after 60 years of power. The government is no closer to its Communist goal today than when Lenin first led the Revolution. A wry Russian joke runs, "Under capitalism man exploits man. Under Socialism it's just the opposite."

11

Was it inevitable that Tsarist Russia had to become a police state? Significantly, Russia was the only important European country which changed from a feudal to an industrial society without going through a democratic period. The Industrial Revolution began late in Russia. By the time it started there was no powerful middle class to create a democratic revolution. So Russia went directly from one totalitarian regime, Tsarism, to another, Communism. The masses of people were used to being controlled and manipulated from above.

Another factor was the fatal weakness of the democratic Kerenski regime that first replaced Tsarist rule. Helpless to satisfy workers' demands for higher wages and peasants' demands for land, it was also powerless to control runaway inflation, feed the hungry or end the hated Russian participation in the war. The people, desperate for an end to their misery, quickly lost patience with any slow democratic road to a better life.

In contrast, speedy and decisive action was promised by the Bolsheviks. They provided leaders who had a dynamic ability to get things done directly. Although they were only a small faction, the secrets of their strength and influence were the dedication and obedience of their tightly disciplined party members, as well as their use of terror and brutality.

"The strength of the working class is organization," Lenin observed before the Revolution. "Without organization the mass of the proletariat is nothing. Organized it is everything." He declared that if 40,000 landlords could rule Russia, as they did under the Tsar, then so could 40,000 Bolsheviks.

Russian idealists who supported the early Bolsheviks believed that they would be building a new world, not only in Russia but everywhere. A world without prisons, hunger, poverty, war or cruel police. The Soviet Union was a gigantic experiment by Lenin and Trotsky to create a model state for that new world. Whether it might actually have developed into a model state in time, had they remained at the controls rather than being supplanted by Stalin, will always remain one of history's more fascinating speculations.

But even if it had, the weakness of the police state is that the quality of its government depends almost entirely on the personality of its leader or leaders. In a democracy, on the other hand, even the worst leader cannot erase the laws of the nation, nor escape the challenge of new elections.

No police state willingly surrenders its powers to the people it rules, and the Soviet Union is no exception. Life has gradually improved for its citizens from a material standpoint, and will probably continue to improve further. But the price they will pay is a continued absence of the freedom we in the Western democracies enjoy, short of an unlikely second Russian Revolution in the foreseeable future.

IV

The Chinese Way

For centuries Chinese peasant farmers lived a bleak, cruel existence, mercilessly mistreated by landlords who fattened on their misery by taking up to 90% of their crops in rent. Slaughtered by raiding warlords, they also died by the millions of flood and famine, driven from their homes to seek survival on tree leaves, roots and wild grass. Malnutrition was so widespread that millions frequently lacked the strength to plant or plow their lands.

Fu Hai-tsao was five when his family was thrown out of their Heng-shan farm home in Hunan for nonpayment of rent during the famine of 1928. They were forced to beg on the roads for food. Fu's father died of starvation while collecting firewood to sell and gathering elm leaves for his family to eat.

"That is my earliest memory," Fu recalled. "Of always being hungry, and Father lying there dead on the road."

During that famine 2 million persons died of hunger in one province alone, and 400,000 children were sold into slavery by their families for food.

During the 19th and early 20th centuries, when foreign powers invaded and occupied parts of China, the Chinese were exploited as cheap labor for the mines, factories and plantations owned by foreign capitalists. Workers labored up to 16 hours a day, 7 days a week, in miserable conditions. When they grew desperate enough to strike, they were beaten with clubs and dispersed by the gunfire of British armies of occupation.

The contempt in which they were held by the Western powers was manifested by signs erected in city parks and other areas they controlled: "Forbidden to dogs and Chinese."

But most Chinese lived in the countryside, peasants whose greatest dream was to own farms of their own, free and clear of their Chinese landlords. Education was too much to hope for. Schooling was for the few, the rich. Only sons of officials, landlords and merchants were given the opportunity to escape illiteracy and "become somebody." Those with education used their knowledge for their own profit.

Chinese peasants and workers were filled with hope in October 1911 when the imperial Manchu government, a pawn to the foreign powers of England, France, Russia, Japan, Germany, Portugal and the United States, was overthrown by revolutionaries who acknowledged one of their own, Sun Yatsen, as their leader. Sun established a Republic of China. Had the recognition and aid he sought from the Western democracies been forthcoming, the whole future history of China might have been different, and China today might have become one of the world's great democracies.

But American and European industrialists preferred doing business with Chinese warlords, who took bribes for letting them do whatever they wanted to in China. As the price of recognition of his new republic, Sun Yatsen was forced to step aside in favor of warlord Yüan Shih-k'ai, former chief adviser to the Manchu throne. When Yüan sought to establish a new dynasty of his own, Sun broke with him and set up a rival Nationalist regime called the Kuomintang.

Upon Yüan's death, the provinces of China fell under the rule of rival warlords, whose armies fought each other for the privilege of milking the people. Sun Yatsen appealed to the West for support of the Kuomintang as the one hope of uniting China under the flag of the Republic. In vain.

Sun turned to the one noncapitalist nation which World War I had brought into the world—the Soviet Union. Lenin and Trotsky, interested in spreading the Communist revolution abroad, gave Sun the help he needed and trained his aide, Chiang Kai-shek, as the leader of the Kuomintang's Nationalist Army. Members of the Chinese Communist party were ordered by Moscow to join and support the Kuomintang.

Sun Yatsen strove to defeat the warlords, unify China and establish a people's government. But conditions under the warlords grew increasingly chaotic. Desperation drove Chinese workers and students to strike, boycott and attack foreign interests in China. The death of Sun brought Chiang Kai-shek to leadership of the Kuomintang. Meeting secretly with representatives of the wealthy merchant class, Chiang made a deal to win their financial support.

Chiang Kai-shek's share of the bargain was revealed in 1929 when he suddenly turned on the Communists within the Kuomintang, massacring tens of thousands. The Communists, led by peasant-born Mao Tse-tung, fought free of the Nationalists in 1935.

Making a historic "Long March" of 7,000 miles that took over a year, they reached the remote mountain base of Yenan, established a Soviet Republic, and made their homes and workshops in caves dug out of the mountains. Here they stood off both the powerful Nationalist armies of Chiang's Kuomintang government, which were now augmented by the warlords' forces, and invading armies sent by Japan.

Led by Mao and his chief aide, Chou En-lai, the Communists called for all of China to unite with them in fighting a war of national liberation against the Japanese, who invaded Manchuria in 1931. Chiang persisted in blockading and attacking only the Chinese Communists, while the Japanese armies swept over China.

Mao and Chou sought to rally the people behind them by winning the trust and support of the peasantry, who hated Chiang's cruel warlord troops. The Chinese Red Army helped the peasants with their harvests, never stole from nor attacked them, and executed wealthy landlords who persecuted them. Explaining the executions, Mao said dryly, "Revolution is not the same thing as inviting people to tea."

Under his leadership, the ranks of the revolutionists swelled rapidly. Peasants were impressed with the discipline drilled into Red Army soldiers, whose leaders were constantly reminded of the Communist slogan "Serve the people."

Everything the Red Army could do to alleviate the age-old misery and wretched conditions of the peasantry was done. At the same time the peasants were grateful for the Red Army's skillful guerrilla warfare against the Japanese troops, who were burning, looting, raping and killing without mercy.

Most Chinese were thrilled by the spectacle of enthusiastic young Red warriors who sang as they marched, who respected the daughters and property of villagers, who slept in streets and fields rather than taking over peoples' homes and who brought justice with them against the hated landlords. In each zone they occupied, they helped the peasant masses.

Their behavior was all the more remarkable in contrast with the troops of Chiang, whose warlord officers were notoriously corrupt, brutal and interested only in plunder.

Chinese students clamored for an end to Nationalist attacks on the Communists, and a top-to-bottom reform of the Kuomintang party. But Chiang saw the Communists as a threat to his military dictatorship, and tried to prevent the students' appeal from reaching the people. Students who demonstrated were clubbed, fired upon, arrested and murdered. Attacking universities, the Nationalists destroyed classrooms and stripped them of "disloyal" books. Students by the tens of thousands fled north to Yenan to join the Communists.

The Communists, meanwhile, insisted that they were not primarily interested in revolution but in fighting a war of national liberation. They expressed willingness to join with all groups in a democratic United Front to drive the Japanese out of China. Criticizing the Kuomintang, Red Army leader Chu Teh declared, "We must have democracy, and democracy doesn't mean secret police, dictatorships, tortures, murders and the disappearance of people everywhere."

2

The Japanese attack on Pearl Harbor in December 1941 made the United States an ally of China in World War II. Washington recognized Chiang's Kuomintang as the government of China. American military and financial aid was rushed to the Nationalists to help them stop the Japanese advance in Asia. But Chiang hoarded this aid to destroy the Communist forces instead. Let *American* military power fight the Japanese!

Turning a deaf ear to Mao's continued appeals for unity and a democratic coalition government, Chiang spurned any cooperation with "Red bandits." He also tried to keep American correspondents and military observers from reaching the Soviet Republic at Yenan. But they managed to get through Chiang's blockade to investigate Chinese Communist operations.

G. Mareel Hall, an American banker in Peking, escaped from advancing Japanese through territory held by the Communist guerrillas. The partisans, he reported, had the enthusiastic support of the peasantry because of "their own incorruptibility and honesty, their energetic patriotism, their devotion to practical democracy."

"The work which we Communists are carrying on today," claimed Yenan's newspaper, *Liberation Daily*, "is the very same work which was carried on earlier in America by Washington, Jefferson and Lincoln." Mao told American Embassy secretary John S. Service, "We will not be afraid of democratic American influence; we welcome it. . . . We will be interested in the most rapid possible development of the country . . . raising the living standard of the people. . . . We must cooperate and we must have American help."

Most Western correspondents were, indeed, impressed by the democratic spirit they found in the Communist camp. Generals and privates lived and were treated alike. The peasants were allowed to participate in governing Communist-held regions.

"Never in Chinese history had the people been so personally and systematically taken into account in the processes of government," reported U.S. Embassy official John Paton Davies. "While this was not democracy in the American sense, the people were truly the nourishing water in which the Communists swam." He agreed with most American observers in Yenan that the Communists, not Chiang, were the wave of China's future.

When World War II was over, civil war erupted between the Communist and Nationalist forces. Both sides rushed to take over cities, territories and arms from the defeated Japanese.

The United States made a serious tactical blunder. Instead of recognizing that the Communists had the overwhelming support of the Chinese masses, Washington failed either to support them or remain neutral. Instead, it increased aid to Chiang's Nationalists, who were now widely hated and feared by the Chinese people.

During the fierce civil war, thousands of landlords were killed by Chinese peasants to avenge ancient wrongs, and to distribute their lands among the landless. Reinforced by huge enlistments, the Chinese Communists' Red Army rolled southward, sweeping aside the corrupt, demoralized Nationalist forces. Even as Chiang's armies crumbled, his officers spent most of their time trying to steal troop payrolls and sell Army supplies on the black market for personal profit.

The Chinese Communists drove Chiang and his Nationalists out of the mainland to refuge on the adjacent island of Formosa (Taiwan). On October 1, 1949, Mao proclaimed the establishment of the People's Republic of China.

At that moment, in the eyes of the Chinese masses, they had been liberated from feudal slavery. They were not sure what to expect from the new government. But how much worse could it be than the rule of the Manchu dynasty? Of the warlords? Of Chiang's Kuomintang? Of Japanese conquerors?

3

The Communists sought to build a totally organized society in which every segment of the people would play an assigned role, as part of a master plan to create a new China. It took Mao and Chou five years to develop a government capable of operating on its own authority without military backup.

Copying many of the methods that had been tested by the Soviet Union over thirty years, the Communists began changing the face of China rapidly through discipline and determination. What they lacked in machine power they made up in manpower, mobilizing the Chinese masses in huge plans to create a modern society.

Unlike the Soviet Union, they sought to win popular cooperation by emphasizing increases in food, textiles and other consumer goods before developing a heavy industry. By first raising the standard of living, they reasoned, they could win the support of the masses for the sacrifices all would have to make to industrialize the nation. The USSR took a dim view of Chinese "heresy" in refusing to copy the Russian priority in Five-Year Plans.

The feudal land system was destroyed by confiscating the properties of the landlords and dividing them up among poor peasants. The distribution averaged something like one and a half acres per peasant, far too small a holding for an adequate farm—but more land than 80% of the people had ever owned. The government later ordered them to pool their small holdings into larger collective farms, jointly owned.

Former landowners not considered guilty of crimes against the people—cruelty to tenant farmers or collaboration with the Japanese—were allowed to join the collectives. Many wealthy landowners, however, were seized and publicly tried with a whole village serving as judge and jury. Tens of thousands were executed. Among them were some smaller landowners falsely accused of crimes by neighbors greedy to share in their property. The transition from feudal to collective farming was frequently savage and bloody.

But in late January 1949 a foreign correspondent in Peking observed, "There is no doubt in my mind that the Communists come here with the bulk of the people on their side. As one walks the streets, the new feeling of relief and relaxation can definitely be sensed."

At first everything was run by the People's Liberation Army (PLA). Interviewing its leaders, Spanish journalist Julio Alvarez reported, "That army bore no resemblance to any other army in the world. It was the people in uniform. It was the army of the least militaristic country in the world."

The Communists were concerned with what the people thought and felt. How could a new Communist society be built, Mao asked, without the full support of the masses? To get that support, he appealed to the 700 million Chinese for their understanding and cooperation. Self-interest had to be put aside as all worked hard and long, not for personal gain, but for the welfare of all. Never before in Chinese history had the people been so motivated.

In this bold experiment to change human nature, Communist

70

party members were directed to set an example by denying themselves rest, food and comfort in an all-out effort to make community projects succeed. Propagandists drummed home the motto "Serve the people." By a form of national "brainwashing," all Chinese were "reeducated" to respect only those who made heroic, self-sacrificing efforts for the common good.

All the benefits that accrued to the people from this program were designed to reinforce their loyalty to Communist ideals.

Newspapers, wall posters and village radio loudspeakers carried on a ceaseless propaganda campaign urging the people to work for the building of the new China. Foreign democratic governments deplored methods such as "thought control." Peking, which did not want its weaknesses or mistakes trumpeted to the world, restricted the ability of foreign correspondents to learn and report what was going on. And to keep Chinese thoughts "pure," all world news reaching China was censored.

One of the problems the Chinese Communists had to cope with was the ancient Chinese family system, which held family ties to be a person's strongest bonds. All loyalty and obedience were due to the head of the family. But how could devotion to the state be uppermost in the mind of every Chinese, if it was overshadowed by the bonds of family? So the government deliberately sought to dissolve those bonds, as part of reshaping the whole structure of Chinese society.

Students were taught to denounce their fathers publicly as practitioners of the old ways, as well as to confess their own shortcomings as citizens of the new China.

The standards of the government in Peking, and of Chairman Mao, became the standards for all China. The whole country was required to master the Chinese dialect called Mandarin, which Mao spoke, and which became known as "ordinary speech." Although China was roughly as wide as the United States, with the same three-hour time differential, all Chinese were required to set their watches by Peking time. Mao, who all his life had been a nonconformist, ironically required a degree of conformism among the Chinese people greater than that demanded by any other nation in the world, including the Soviet Union.

4

The Chinese knew they could expect little help from the United States. They were not surprised when Washington blockaded their country after the Communists came to power. So Peking turned for help to the Soviet Union, which at that time was in a friendly mood toward its Asian neighbor. The Russians sent raw materials, technicians and skilled workers to reconstruct a China devastated by war and civil war. At first the Chinese closely followed the Soviet model of industrial development. Able students, they learned all they could from the Russian experts.

Lacking machinery, tools and capital, they made the most of their richest resource, manpower. Armies of men, working with little but bare hands, labored mightily to build dams, factories, earthen dikes and other huge projects. Lacking tractors and trucks, they moved great loads by harnessing themselves as beasts of burden. The new China was built by a stupendous mass effort that some described as voluntary slavery to bring about a better life for the Chinese and their children.

One sign of this better life was a National Health Congress held in August 1950. It began a huge program of preventive medicine to wipe out epidemic diseases. Medical care was broadened to serve the masses of peasants, workers, soldiers and students.

Mao relied on regimentation to implement his plans. The Chinese were organized into work teams in factories and on agricultural communes. For the nation's defenses, he also mobilized every person in the society, even small children of both sexes, in local militia exercises that taught them how to use guerrilla warfare against any invaders.

All were remolded in their thinking according to Maoist policy: "If we have shortcomings, we are not afraid to have them pointed out and criticized, because we serve the people. Anyone, no matter who, may point out our shortcomings. If he is right, we will correct them."

The Communists mounted a nationwide campaign to have workers, students, soldiers and peasants criticize each other in "struggle" sessions—meetings in which all were expected to struggle against the "errors" or "reactionary tendencies" which kept a Chinese from becoming an ideal citizen of a Communist society. Each person was expected to acknowledge his own shortcomings as well, as a sign of penitence and determination to reform. Thus, intensive and persistent criticism was seen as the tool of constant improvement.

In effect, this program of thought control tended to make the Chinese feel guilt and shame for personal feelings—normal in our own society—which lead people to pursue their own advantage. The Communists also used struggle sessions to confiscate any hoarded wealth. Anyone found with hidden assets was often accused of various crimes by his associates and acquaintances, out of fear of otherwise being "struggled" against themselves. The authorities sometimes tortured an accused man until he confessed. He would then be fined the exact amount of his hoarded wealth.

Mao sought to develop a strong sense of national unity that would make all Chinese work together harmoniously. To that end he attempted to bridge the cultural gap that separated learned officials and scholars from the illiterate masses. He also sought to wipe out distinctions between city and country people, brain workers and manual workers, factory workers and peasants. No privileged economic class was allowed to develop. Instead a classless society was built in which all were supposed to advance together, side by side.

Mao set the example by mingling with the humblest peasants, squatting with them in the fields to talk about crop conditions and ask their advice on how to improve harvests.

Many Chinese disliked the regimentation and sacrifices the government imposed upon them, but dared not protest. Mao allowed no basic criticism of the Communist party. He was shaken when in 1956 Khrushchev denounced Stalin, revealing that the Soviet taboo on criticism of the government had hidden many terrible deeds by the Russian dictator.

Khrushchev's exposé had led to a riot in Poland, an uprising in Hungary, and serious unrest in Eastern Europe. Mao worried lest similar eruptions manifest themselves in China, too. He decided to give the Chinese a safety valve which would let the dissatisfied blow off steam harmlessly.

A "Hundred Flowers" campaign was begun with the slogan "Let a hundred flowers bloom and let a hundred schools of thought contend." But Mao was stunned by the criticism that came pouring through the opened floodgates. It was directed not merely at minor mistakes, but at the Communist party and at the authority of Mao himself. Many Chinese complained of the lack of freedom and democracy.

The Hundred Flowers campaign was abruptly canceled, replaced by a new campaign which emphasized the dangers of "Rightist thinking." Many of those who had voiced or written serious criticisms were punished. One teacher was sent to work as a railway coolie, and another was demoted to school janitor with no one permitted to speak to him. Many professional people were sentenced to "labor reform"—manual labor on farm cooperatives.

Although China was now a police state, Mao was no Stalin murdering 10 million rebellious kulaks in order to impose collective farming on the Soviet Union. Mao used persuasion and propaganda, not wholesale brute force, to transform private farming into communal agriculture.

He did it a step at a time. Peasants were first shown the advantages of sharing manpower, tools and animals. By 1956 nearly all Chinese farmers had joined cooperatives, holding their own land privately but working it jointly with other lands and sharing profits.

The peasants were next induced to join their holdings in collective farms, owned by members in common. By 1958, the year of Mao's proclaimed "Great Leap Forward," the collective farms were amalgamated into communes. These were self-sufficient, huge farm complexes with their own factories, schools, water-control projects and health centers. As first conceived, the communes were failures. After some trial, error and modifications, however, they became permanent fixtures of Chinese society. They represent an important aspect of Mao's dream of erasing differences between country and city.

Millions of urban dwellers left the cities to join the communes. Peasants, in turn, were torn out of *their* traditional roles, becoming industrial workers, builders and engineering hands as well as farmers.

The government also extended the Great Leap Forward to the

educational system, requiring university students to complete four years of academic work in two. At the same time students were expected to volunteer to combine mornings of study with afternoons of productive labor. On factory assembly lines, where loudspeakers blared out constant exhortations to work faster, students and workers who fell behind were singled out for criticism over the public address system.

Students compelled to do agricultural work spent 13 hours a day in the field, often working by lamplight, on a daily ration of cabbage soup and a bowl of rice. They were often resented by the peasants because the hungry students ate some of the food they harvested while at work.

To make sure that university students developed the correct Communist attitude, classes were often suspended for political discussions. The old society of China was contrasted with the new. One student who hated these sessions as obvious attempts at thought control described what they were like:

"The idea was that in the comparison of the old and new society, you had lapsed in your awareness of the vast superiority of the new over the old. As a result you had made errors in your thinking and acting. You confessed these errors to your fellow group members, who accused you of additional errors you had neglected to mention. You were criticized severely for this. In the end, you begged forgiveness, you promised to strive harder to reform yourself and you gave unstinting praise to the Party and Chairman Mao."

The Great Leap Forward was an ambitious undertaking which bogged down in the communes because of unrealistic expectations. The factories, manned by too high a percentage of unskilled workers, had low productivity. The quality of tractors produced was poor, with constant breakdowns and a shortage of spare parts that forced them to stand idle. Raw materials failed to arrive when expected. Bottlenecks developed everywhere.

The government sought to inspire worker enthusiasm with propaganda posters on factory walls, reminding them that former slaves were now owners of the property of their former masters.

The Chinese were taught that their leader was infallible. If Chairman Mao said something was true, it was true. Hadn't he said so himself? Not that Mao was a vainglorious man. He forbade the naming of any province, city or town after him, and banned birthday celebrations in his honor. He did not, however, attempt to stop the use of his picture in every nook and cranny of China, along with banners singing his praises. He once explained that it was necessary to Chinese unity and patriotism for the people to have a symbol around whom they could rally.

If the Great Leap Forward left much to be desired as an attempt to industrialize an abysmally backward nation in a hurry, it was even more disastrous as an agricultural program. Especially when unfavorable weather conditions almost caused a famine. Mass starvation was avoided only by strict rationing and emergency shipments of grain from regions with a surplus.

There were reports that as many as 70,000 people starved to death in Kansu province, because the Communist party secretary there tried to conceal conditions from Peking in order to make a good impression. Many refugees tried to flee to the British colony of Hong Kong to escape a winter of hunger.

5

The agricultural failure of the Great Leap Forward was a stunning blow to Mao, hurting his prestige within the Chinese Communist party. The Central Committee edged Mao's supporters out of positions of leadership, replacing them with leaders Mao distrusted. The fact that he felt helpless to prevent these changes indicated that he did not exercise sole dictatorial power in China. His political rivals, the conservatives within the party, had power comparable to his own. They controlled most of the day-by-day machinery of the government—the mass media, the trade unions, the youth organizations and the school system.

Growing increasingly angry at what he called the "authority faction," Mao accused leading bureaucrats of corrupting the revolutionary spirit of the people. Was this not a gross betrayal of the Revolution he and his followers had brought about at a staggering sacrifice of lives and great suffering?

In the spring of 1966 he unleashed a "Cultural Revolution," turning to the masses for support in purging the bureaucracy and destroying their "revisionist" system. Fearful that the new generation of Chinese was growing up soft and complacent, he also sought to revitalize "the revolutionary consciousness of the people."

Part of his plan called for "reeducation" of all officials in a supervisory position. They were sent to live and work with the masses every third year, to identify with the aspirations of the people, not try to rise above them.

Mao closed schools and universities for a year to let young "Red Guards" mount a crusade in imitation of his Long March of 1935. They swept across the country putting up wall posters urging the people to be faithful to the principles of the Revolution. What excitement! Tens of thousands of people were beaten up by the zealous Red Guards as "reactionary elements."

The uproar was so great that many foreign governments imagined Mao had gone mad. Would Red China collapse under the shock of the upheaval? But Mao still had the firm support of the peasantry, who understood what he was trying to do. Haughty Communist officials were uprooted, and the "revisionist" President, Liu Shao-ch'i, was overthrown in disgrace.

By that time the rebels were uncontrollable.

"Any person who opposes Chairman Mao, however important he may be, will be burned to death!" threatened Red Guard wall posters. The rebels took over newspapers, drove out factory officials and seized political power in many cities. The anarchy finally compelled Mao to let the Red Army be used to hold the Red Guards in check. After some violent clashes, the young rebels were finally subdued and dispersed back to their home towns and universities.

But to a large extent the Cultural Revolution had been successful. It had overthrown many "revisionist" officials of China—those who sought to make Chinese society more middle class. It had also shaken loose many traditionalist Chinese families from their reverence for the "Four Olds"—old thought, old culture, old manners and old customs. Reminded forcibly of their revolutionary traditions, the Chinese were driven to adhere to Mao's "Yenan style—hard work and plain living."

"My eldest boy is fourteen years old," one Chinese said. "He goes to school. One day when I came home I saw that his neck was dirty. It was black with grime. I asked him why. He answered: 'In our school we pupils have decided to live in the Yenan style.' I had to explain to him that being a revolutionary is not the same as no longer washing your neck."

When China's schools were reopened, their emphasis was changed from developing the most advantaged students to expanding educational opportunities for all youngsters from peasant and working-class families. Examination systems were "reformed" by having the poorest students taking exams shown the answers in advance—"so that everyone in the class can produce ideal work," Mao explained.

Between 1968 and 1971 the Chinese government was restructured to provide greater local control, with the people given an increased voice in their own affairs. New administrative "revolutionary committees" and new Communist party committees were elected in all provinces, dominated by the local military. The new system was still a long cry from democracy, but it did make for less authoritarian government.

In 1975 Mao, then 82, was approaching death. While secure in his post as the venerated idol of China, he seemed less powerful than he had once been. "They don't listen to me much anymore," he complained of China's other leaders.

When Mao died in September 1976, a struggle for power ensued between the moderate and radical factions of the Chinese Communist party. The Politburo selected as the new Chairman of the party the man Mao had chosen as the new Premier when Chou En-lai had died, Hua Kuo-feng. A moderate, Hua moved swiftly to arrest Mao's widow, Chiang Ching, and three radical colleagues. Assailed as the "gang of four," they were accused of "towering crimes"—notably, driving Mao to his grave and plotting to "usurp party and state power" through a coup. Fighting broke out in some cities, but the Army, loyal to Hua, suppressed it.

Soon after taking office, Hua indicated that under him China would pursue a calmer, more moderate course both domestically and in foreign affairs, with emphasis on increased economic development and foreign trade.

6

Is the organization of every aspect of life under the Chinese Communists admirable or deplorable?

"China's achievements in agriculture simply hit you in the eye," observed Norman Borlaug, Nobel Peace Prize-winning scientist. "The people everywhere, both in cities and the countryside, look well fed. You don't see the abject poor and hungry that you see in other parts of the world."

On the other hand visiting Republican Congresswoman Millicent Fenwick of New Jersey declared, "I feel a sense of pity that these wonderful people are caught in the Communist system, and there doesn't seem to be any escape."

One small revealing sidelight on Chinese regimentation was discovered by Australian writer Ross Terrill, who had wondered how China managed the clockwork precision of its huge parades, with every element perfectly timed and in place. Visiting Peking's vast parade ground, Tien An Men Square, he noted that each flat square flagstone had its own number.

Everything, everyone was assigned an exact position for the smooth orchestration of the whole parade, just as everyone and everything was regimented for the planned operation of the Chinese economy. No hit-or-miss, catch-as-catch-can, freedom-of-movement individualism under the banners of the People's Republic!

Inscriptions on Peking's public buildings once identified them with graceful titles like "Pavilion of Pleasant Sounds." Today they bear "educational" inscriptions like "People Alone Are the Motive Force of History." No Chinese is ever very far away from a slogan or Maoist thought to shape his thinking.

But now municipal or provincial governments, rather than remote rule from Peking, shape the everyday life of the Chinese. Places of work, shops, schools, banks, theaters, restaurants, hospitals, newspapers and wall posters are all run by local revolutionary committees.

What would life be like for you today under the Chinese police state?

The extent of your education would depend on where you lived. Not more than 6% of your grade-school class would go on to high school if you lived in the country. Almost all would if you lived in the city. But no more than 2% of your class would reach a university level.

In grade school you would study politics, Chinese, physical training, math, and revolutionary art and culture. As a fifth grader you would also be taught English and "common knowledge," which would include mechanics, agriculture and natural science as applied in school workshops and gardens. If you hoped for a government career, it would also be essential to attend classes in Maoist thought, after school hours.

As a high schooler in Shanghai and its 500 suburbs, you would attend a two-story brick building with crowded classrooms (50 to 60 pupils per class) for 6 hours a day, 6 days a week. Your courses would include politics, Chinese, English, Russian, chemistry, agriculture, history, math, and revolutionary art and literature. You would also spend 30% of your time in "work experience"—manual labor—on a farm or in a school factory, helping turn out products for the consumer market.

You could no longer enter a university directly after graduation from high school, as students did before the Cultural Revolution, by taking and passing entrance exams. You would now first be required to prove your "political consciousness" by working for several years in the army, in factories or on farms, on jobs where you were needed most. Then your acceptance would not depend upon your intelligence or scholarly achievement, or even upon completion of high school, but primarily upon recommendations of the people working in your unit. They must certify that you have a "Red heart"—an excellent record in "serving the people" that makes you deserving of college training.

Chinese university faculties are not particularly happy with this method of selection. Some have even expelled students as unqualified. One professor said, "Today's students are coarse tea mugs that cannot be carved into refined cups." Students at some universities have protested by striking, putting up wall posters accusing the faculty of seeking to restore "revisionist" educational practices.

80

Even if you were not a full-time student, you would probably be attending some kind of adult-education class. The government presses all Chinese to keep studying and training themselves in their spare time to become more effective workers and citizens.

Although the Chinese Communist system has wiped out illiteracy, and given the masses a relatively high level of education for an Asian country, Dorothy Jurney, Assistant Managing Editor of the Philadelphia *Inquirer*, found herself depressed by her visit to Chinese schools and universities.

"Very little if anything in China is spontaneous," she reported, "but the life of the Chinese students is even more regimented than most. . . ." Students study what they are ordered to learn, which "amounts to a vocational trade and revolutionary political thought." She noted that students of Peking University spent half their time in the 7 factories and 27 workshops on campus, and in 65 Peking factories tied in with the university.

As a Chinese worker, you would be assigned to a job and required to remain on it. But a crude form of industrial democracy operates. How well you were paid would depend on the revolutionary committee running your plant—how they regarded your dedication in applying "Maoist thought" to your job, the level of your skill and the number of hours you worked.

Your production quota would be decided by a conference of fellow workers, the revolutionary committee and the local Communist party committee. The party has the last word. If you were dissatisfied, you could protest either by putting up a poster on the factory wall or by voicing your dissatisfaction at a mass assembly for discussion.

While you would be able to criticize officials at your place of work, you would also have to accept criticism by them in turn. Not only for mistakes or shortcomings in your work, but also for defects in your character. A plant manager would have every right to reproach you publicly for being too smug or conceited.

If there were no job opening for you in a local plant, store, office or farm, you would be given work in the massive public employment program that cleans and repairs streets, cares for parks and gardens, or irrigates and reforests the land. These programs, assuring that everyone has a job, are one reason modern China is so immaculate and green.

As a factory worker you could eat in a canteen, where your own mess kit would be filled with healthful, tasty, well-cooked food for a cost of 5¢ to 17¢. You would also have access to a clinic with a large number of beds and a considerable medical staff, free of charge. A fine kindergarten would look after your children.

7

Most Chinese are grateful to the Communists for bringing them a better life than they had previously known. "Before the liberation," said one woman worker, "I used to work at a textile factory. In those days I was often beaten by my superiors and was forced to work day and night. I was not even given time to eat lunch. I had three children, but all died of malnutrition."

A former farmer said, "I just could not make my living by tilling the soil, because the landowner took 70% of the crops I raised. So I went to Shanghai and worked as a coolie. I worked 14 hours a day. . . . I did not have a house to live in, so I slept under a bridge or under the eaves of a building at night. Compared with those days, I live like a king now. . . . The good days came because Chairman Mao did so much to bring about a new age."

If you were a worker on a commune farm, your schedule would be something like this during busy seasons: 4:30 A.M. Everybody rises. Grandmothers tend infants; mothers prepare breakfast. 5–7 A.M. Men and all teenagers work in fields. 7–8 A.M. Breakfast for all. 8 A.M.–Noon. Babies to commune nurseries; children to brigade schools; men, women and older children to fields. Noon–3:30 P.M. Lunch, and rest for all except wives, who wash and hang laundry. 3:30–8 P.M. School or work in fields for all. Wives return home an hour earlier to cook supper and attend to children. 8–10 P.M. Supper and brigade activities, adult classes, cultural performances or fraternizing. Leisure mostly for men; women attend to children and put them to bed.

Career opportunities for women in China, however, are steadily increasing, even though most high positions in Chinese society today are still filled by men. Women now make up about a fourth of all scientific workers; many are becoming administrators.

As a commune worker, your pay would depend upon your skill, your physical strength, how hard and long you work. Members assemble once a month to discuss and establish each other's ratings. Shares in the commune's profits are divided accordingly. You would be able to supplement yours from private sales of your own garden produce.

Non-Chinese aboriginals make up 6% of China's population, living primarily in remote border regions. The Communists have been careful to respect minority cultures, while absorbing them into Chinese society. Peking encourages migration of Chinese into these regions, ensuring their welcome by sending along experts in forestry, agriculture and animal husbandry to help make deserts and frozen prairies flourish. New towns are built around old villages, giving minorities their first hospitals, schools and industries.

Discrimination is forbidden. Minority children are given preference in the universities. Illiteracy has been wiped out among aboriginal adults. Chinese immigrants intermarry freely with minority Chinese. "We began to get our schools and to change our life and the old witchcraft disappeared," reported a native of the Singpho tribe. He added proudly, "I myself have married a Chinese girl."

In 1959, however, Peking encountered resistance to its Five-Year Plans in Tibet, an isolated region of priest-exploited serfs. When the Dalai Lama's priests led an armed revolt, some 65,000 Tibetans were slaughtered by the Chinese People's Liberation Army. Another 43,000 fled to India with the Dalai Lama. Buddhist monasteries were shut down, and their lands distributed among the peasants.

Cultural life in China tends to be on the dull side. Most entertainment is loaded with indoctrination intended to inspire feelings of patriotism, Communist fervor and hatred for the Bad Old Days. Just as the Soviet Union did, Mao insisted that films, plays, art and literature had to serve as "weapons of Socialism," or else be considered "decadent."

They tend to bore younger Chinese, however. Recently a Canton theater screened a new film showing how the Communists had won the hearts and minds of the Chinese people during the civil war period. When the hero's pale face was shown crimsoning with fiery determination as he glimpsed a portrait of Mao, the younger members of the audience burst into sarcastic laughter.

Although legally entitled to free time for leisure, rest and recreation, as a Chinese you would be under subtle pressure to give up large chunks of it to study and do volunteer work of benefit to commune or community. You would be aware that like everyone else, you would be under party observation. If you were reported as a "lagging-behind element," you would be expected to confess your sins and mend the error of your ways. If you did not, you would find yourself socially ostracized. Or worse, publicly humiliated at a mass "struggle" meeting where you and other balky individualists would be "struggled against"—denounced as bad citizens.

The power of a "Big Brother" police state to make you feel evil, worthless and ashamed unless you do what is expected of you is enormous. So whether you felt like it or not, you would probably make sure to spend enough Sundays building a dam, planting trees in the countryside, putting on a factory concert, assisting a widower left with four small children, or whatever. Such altruism would also help your record when you were considered for promotion or vacation benefits.

Most socializing is done not at home but around pots of tea in public places. Not only are homes too small, but the ears of neighbors who might be eavesdropping are too big. "Since plotting is suspected everywhere," noted French journalist Jules Roy remarked, "intimacy no longer exists. . . . No one ever talks unless there are witnesses present, so that no one else can cast suspicion on his view, and notes are taken on everything so that there will be visible proof of what was said."

8

You would be careful especially about contacts with foreigners that were not authorized. China is still a closed society, despite improved relations with the West. The authorities discourage all but token conversation between Chinese and foreigners, particularly newsmen and embassy personnel.

Despite the détente with America that began in 1972, the Chinese learn only the negative aspects of life in America, making them feel how fortunate they are to live in China. Communist intellectuals defend distortions of the outside world in the Chinese news media as a necessary weapon in the class struggle. "Only the things that serve the party cause in the class struggle are right and true," one told Swedish journalist Sven Lindqvist. "There is no other truth. . . . You think that you can report what you have seen and heard without considering which class is going to gain or lose by it. That's a delusion." If you didn't choose to write as an instrument of Communism, weren't you playing the capitalist game?

With the now-sanctified views of Mao drilled into you day after day, you would soon begin to know them by rote and accept them as gospel. It would only be one step from that belief to crediting the generalities of Maoist thought for specific achievements in every phase of everyday life.

"By applying the thoughts of Chairman Mao, we grow bigger vegetables," insisted one commune team leader. Had not Chairman Mao taught us to work together and help each other? To examine facts and not follow old ideas blindly? To experiment and learn from the results? Then had not Mao helped us to grow bigger vegetables by such methods?

Mao had worried that without constant prodding, the revolutionary fervor of his people would ebb, and China would once more become divided between privileged bureaucrats and the masses. Already some of the leveling effects of the Cultural Revolution have been undone. Many party officials and army officers and their families travel around in limousines to shop. Further evidence of the relaxation of revolutionary discipline can be seen in the willingness of hotel workers and others to accept tips—considered a capitalist form of degradation—in the form of pens and cigarette lighters.

In November 1974 some intellectuals, led by Canton Art Academy graduate Li Cheng-fu, indicated their dissatisfaction with the shortcomings of Communism by writing and distributing wall posters and mimeographed copies of their criticism. Labeling these "extraordinarily reactionary and malicious," Vice Premier Li

Hsien-nien ordered the ringleaders arrested, criticized and "struggled against."

There were undeniable pockets of discontent in the broad support for the Chinese Communists' paternalistic brand of police state. In September 1975 work stoppages protesting low wages and poor working and living conditions were reported in the coal, steel and railway industries. Troops had to be sent to Hangchow to quiet disturbances, and many workers were sent to "labor camps" for "reeducation"—an ordeal in thought control.

One former labor-camp prisoner, Bao Ruo-wang, managed to smuggle out an account of his experience. He charged that prisoners were fed rotten potato peelings, paper pulp, praying mantis eggs and undigested corn kernels salvaged from horse manure. Hunger reduced him from 191 pounds to 93, and miserable living conditions gave him boils and tuberculosis.

According to Bao, the system called for a prisoner to confess his misdeed, only to have other prisoners accuse him of lying: "After three or four days the victim begins inventing sins he has never committed. After a week he is prepared to go to any lengths. It is one of the most effective weapons . . . to control his thoughts." Prisoners were not allowed to speak to each other of personal subjects, or to cry.

The "public security service," which allegedly protects the state against the sabotage of "counterrevolutionaries," has the power to arrest suspects and confine them in labor reform camps without trial, for indefinite periods. The government has stated, "Only a small minority, perhaps 5%, is against us; these are being forced to build Socialism." According to Bao Ruo-wang, an estimated 16 million Chinese men and women are in labor camps or prisons.

The government stirred up a hornet's nest of opposition by forcing young city people to perform manual labor in rural areas. Many youths sent to the countryside vanished and went underground, joining a "Red Youth Society" that survives by theft.

Each year a number of determined Chinese, mostly young, attempt the perilous swim across the treacherous Mirs Bay from Communist China to Hong Kong. Many are drowned, their bodies swept out to sea by strong currents. Few who reach the British crown colony are allowed to remain. Most refugees end up back in a Chinese internment camp, where they are interrogated, forced to confess their sins and disciplined by months of hard labor under careful surveillance.

Change of heart, rather than punishment, is the basic aim of Chinese Communist justice. Mao always held that a reformed sinner who has "seen the error of his ways" is of more use to society than a caged, unrepentant prisoner, who remains a threat to it.

Often village justice does not bother to use courts or laws. When a commune team leader near Kunming was discovered to be embezzling funds from his team, he was criticized at a village meeting and forced to criticize himself and promise never to steal again. Expelled from the party—which cost him a loss of prestige and a leadership position—he also had to pay back the stolen sum. Comparing this concept of justice to the Soviet idea, one Chinese explained, "The Soviets shot too many people. You don't cure corruption that way. Then nobody wants to correct the neighbor who is stealing the common funds. Violence ought to be used sparingly."

Likewise, few Chinese policemen arrest or give summonses to people for minor misdemeanors. The offenders are given instead a lecture on the duties of citizenship in a Communist society. A petty thief taken to court would receive only a modest fine or a jail sentence up to only 15 days. On the other hand, the penalty for narcotics violations is death. The Communists abhor that era of Chinese history when Western imperialists corrupted the Chinese people by importing and encouraging the use of opium.

In the cities, if a Chinese is arrested his case will usually be heard by a court made up of a judge and two jurors elected by the people. Jurors as well as judge have a right to question the defendant, who is allowed defense counsel as well as the right to have relatives, friends and members of the organizations he belongs to testify as to his character. If he is found guilty and sentenced to a prison or labor camp, the government will provide aid to his family if it is needed.

Chinese justice often represents decisions arrived at by personal judgments of the court, rather than according to specific laws as in the West. It is nevertheless successful in keeping China's crime rate remarkably low. Chinese and foreign visitors can go anywhere without being victimized by robbers, hoodlums, muggers or rapists. Chinese who find lost items invariably return them to their owners.

Perhaps much of the credit must go to the Chinese themselves, who have had a long tradition as a peaceable, honest and law-abiding people.

9

In evaluating China as a police state, it is necessary to dispense with some myths promulgated by those hostile to, or ignorant of, documented reports about the Chinese Communists by impartial Western sinologists.

One must acknowledge that the great mass of Chinese people are considerably better off under their government today than they ever were before the Revolution. Pockets of discontent exist, but it is a mistake to imagine that most Chinese are eager to revolt against their authoritarian government in order to obtain Western-style freedom and civil liberties.

Most Chinese feel that they are cared for, considered, given a voice in their lives—participants in building a great new Communist society that belongs to them.

Many in the West see such convictions as the result of "brainwashing." Are the Chinese blind to the shortcomings of Communist rule? Credulous about the extent to which they are permitted to control their own lives? According to China's leaders, the Chinese masses see the quality of their lives more clearly and correctly than the "capitalist roaders."

"Whether you call it 'brainwashing' or the transformation of one's world outlook," declared Central Committee member Yao Wenyuan, "what we are talking about is the same . . . the transformation of one's own ideology."

By getting hundreds of millions of Chinese to think alike, in unity and harmony, the Communist leaders have been able to organize them into a great battalion of workers to build new factories, agricultural complexes, schools, hospitals and homes. Enlisting this dedication and energy by unceasing exhortation, the leaders were able to build a vast force that has transformed the face of the nation. Mistakes and setbacks have not prevented gradual progress.

In their favor must also be counted the building of a united China with no warlords or bandits; food for all and flood control in a land with a history of terrible famine and floods; great cleanliness in villages and cities; honesty of most officials; a spirit of mutual help and cooperation fostered among the people, along with a dedication to work and study.

Against the Chinese police state, however, must be charged extreme intolerance of opposite points of view by the party leaders, with dissenters held up to public scorn and banished to forced-labor camps. Also the crushing of the spirit of individuality by insistence upon conformism. Severe press censorship that allows citizens to read only what the government wants them to know. And a humorless, overserious approach to life which tends to make existence in China a dull and colorless business.

For most older Chinese, however, these faults are offset by the great changes brought about by the government for those who were once poor and oppressed, insulted and injured. "In the old society, who would respect us ordinary working people?" asked the leader of a Shanghai retired-workers' cultural group.

Civil liberties have little meaning to most Chinese.

Significantly, it was the Father of the Revolution, Dr. Sun Yatsen, who declared, "The Chinese know nothing of liberty." Shielded from a full understanding of the outside world, most Chinese have little interest in a political liberty that has never been part of their history. "While at sea," urged one Chinese Communist slogan, "put your trust in the helmsman; in government, place your trust in Mao Tse-tung."

One American visitor tried to make a Chinese understand the value of our Fifth Amendment, which gives American citizens the right to refuse to testify against themselves in criminal proceedings. But how could a person improve, protested the puzzled Chinese, and how could mistakes be detected and corrected, unless everyone first confessed error?

For most Chinese, freedom means the freedom to make a living from the land or from a job; the freedom, in short, to exist in a country that they feel now belongs to them. It was in this sense that the Communists called their armed forces the People's Liberation Army—a people's militia to liberate them from the landlords, warlords, merchants and foreign imperialists who had long kept them in servitude.

"This is an honest government," a retired Chinese merchant told American journalist Edgar Snow. "Hard, but honest. It has made China one great country again. Chinese can hold up their heads in the world. We are not foreign slaves anymore. . . . Maybe the government is too strong, sometimes too young to listen to others. But—it does good things for China and does not steal."

The Chinese are reconciled to hardship because they are used to it, because all share it, and because now those who toil are accorded respect and dignity as the most important members of their community and country.

There is little likelihood that the more than 800 million Chinese who now live under a Communist police state will experience any change in their form of government in the foreseeable future. Nor is there any serious indication that most Chinese want it to change.

V

Variations on the Left

When China first turned Communist, Western powers including the United States feared that it would join with the Soviet Union in a huge international Communist alliance that would threaten the capitalist world. But it soon became apparent that their systems were so different, so hostile to each other, that the two Red nations were bitter enemies.

Behind this clash are differences of race, culture and language. The Chinese distrust the Russians as Europeans. The Russians are suspicious of the Chinese as Asians. Each power also disputes the geographical boundary between them. The Chinese fear the Russians may suddenly unleash a nuclear bomb attack against them. The Russians in turn fear that China's vast masses may suddenly swarm across their common border into the Soviet Union's largely empty eastern regions.

Thus the common bond of being Communist police states, rather than making them world partners, has actually united each country more solidly against the other.

There are similar wide variations among the police states of the smaller Communist countries. Some, like Yugoslavia, allow a large degree of personal freedom. Some, like Cuba, operate with the informality of a baseball club. Some, like the Communist satellite governments of Eastern Europe established by the Soviet Union after World War II, have milked their people to satisfy the needs of the Soviet Union.

All Communist countries like to emphasize the "equality" that

Communism has brought to their people. But the record indicates that when a system of privilege was destroyed, the new government often simply shifted all power to a new elite group.

George Orwell satirized this observation in his ironic novel *Animal Farm*, describing how animals revolted and took over operation of their farm. Their leader laid down a single commandment: ALL ANIMALS ARE EQUAL, BUT SOME ANIMALS ARE MORE EQUAL THAN OTHERS.

The countries of Eastern Europe did not turn Communist by revolution, but had Communist governments imposed upon them by the Soviet Red Army. Former Prime Minister of England Winston Churchill made this clear in his famous speech at Fulton, Missouri, on March 5, 1946. "From Stettin in the Baltic to Trieste in the Adriatic an iron curtain has descended across the Continent," he said. "Behind that line lie all the capitals of the ancient States of Central and Eastern Europe—Warsaw, Berlin, Prague, Vienna, Budapest, Belgrade, Bucharest and Sofia. All these famous cities and the populations around them live in the Soviet sphere, and all are subject in one form or another not only to Soviet influence but to a very high and increasing measure of control from Moscow."

At this time there are no Communist governments in Western Europe, although there are strong Communist parties in Italy, France and Portugal. The people of Western Europe have refused to elect them to power for fear they would serve as instruments of the Soviet Union. But these parties have become increasingly independent of Moscow in recent years, and have publicly disagreed with the Russians.

"There cannot be a single [Communist] model valid for all situations," said Enrico Berlinguer, leader of almost two million Italian Communists. He and other Western Communist leaders insist that they seek to come to power or share it only through the ballot. They reject the idea of a police state in favor of democratic methods.

Berlinguer and Georges Marchais, who leads France's Communists, have vowed to protect political freedoms, the rights of other parties, and the right of the people to vote them out of office. Marchais declared that he no longer believes in the Marxist concept of the dictatorship of the proletariat. Socialist party leaders are skeptical. If the Communists really mean it, why haven't they converted to Socialism?

2

It may be useful to examine how and why Communism came to power in smaller countries around the globe, and what the establishment of these Leftist police states has meant to the people who live under them. One notable example is our neighbor Cuba. In 1959 a Marxist government was placed at our doorstep when Fidel Castro overthrew the repressive Right-wing dictatorship of Fulgencio Batista.

A struggle against Batista's Right-wing police state was launched by a group of idealistic youths known as the 26th of July movement. In 1953, led by young lawyer Fidel Castro, they attacked Fort Moncada barracks outside Santiago in the hope of stirring an uprising. But Batista was too powerfully entrenched, the Cuban people too disorganized and fearful of police terrorism. The attack failed. Castro and his followers were jailed, then exiled to Mexico.

He returned secretly in December 1956 at the head of a tiny invasion force of 82 men. A magnetic, dynamic leader, Castro inspired the blind faith of his followers and the poor peasants of Cuba. They saw him as their champion, speaking the language the people wanted to hear. He denounced Batista and militarism, and promised to restore the Cuban constitution of 1940, with free elections, honest government and social democracy. Sharing snake meat and the hardships of mountain life with his men, Castro was trusted by them as incorruptible.

None of this band of revolutionists were Communists, although they were quickly labeled as such both by Batista and the American Ambassador to Cuba. Any of Castro's little band falling into the hands of Batista's police were either shot or tortured for information. As Castro increased his raids, Batista intensified counterterrorism. Some 20,000 Cubans were tortured as suspected sympathizers.

Castro used a guerrilla radio station and newspaper to conduct a skillful propaganda campaign. Recruits and arms poured into his revolutionary movement. His zeal and sense of mission inspired most downtrodden Cubans to see in him a Robin Hood crusading to take from the rich to give to the poor.

Batista's own troops grew increasingly disgusted with the greed and brutality of the dictator. Many deserted to the ranks of the 26th of July movement. When Castro felt strong enough to abandon the hit-and-run tactics of guerrilla warfare, he began a military drive on the capital in Havana. One after the other, towns and villages greeted his revolutionaries with wild enthusiasm.

Castro's forces became an irresistible tide sweeping across Cuba. Batista's troops either fled, surrendered or joined the rebels. Batista himself fled as Castro and his bushy-bearded army of liberation entered Havana in triumph.

Many vengeful liberators, enraged at the tortures that had been inflicted upon their forces and sympathizers by Batista's henchmen, were less than gentle in disposing of all who were caught. Some 600, denounced as war criminals in trials that were essentially legal lynch courts, were executed.

The U.S. State Department was loud in its condemnation. Most Cubans approved of the executions as just punishment.

One of Castro's first acts was to nationalize large land holdings. He divided some into small plots for distribution among tenant farmers; others became state farms. Speeding around the country by jeep, he listened to what the people wanted, and began issuing streams of orders to give it to them.

He denied that he was a Communist. "Our revolution is not Communism," he declared. "Our ideals do not belong to Communist doctrine. The revolution is original. It has its own philosophy, completely its own."

But Castro ignored the question of new elections, introducing more and more reforms by personal decree. The Cuban middle class worried that a Right-wing dictatorship had been replaced by a Left-wing one.

The American CIA tried to assassinate Castro, and at the same time the Kennedy Administration sought to wreck the Cuban economy. Imposing a trade boycott on Cuba, Washington saw to it that most of Latin America supported it.

Castro had not at first been supported by the Cuban Communists, who had denounced him as an "adventurist." In the last few months of the Batista regime, however, when they had realized that Castro's victory was inevitable, they had sided with him. Now, under siege from the powerful United States, he needed Communist help if his revolution was to survive. More particularly, he needed essential supplies from the country the Cuban Communists regarded as their power base.

Turning to the Soviet Union, Castro agreed to bring Cuba into the Communist orbit in exchange for Soviet economic aid and military protection. As part of the deal, the disciplined Cuban Communist party organization united the workers solidly behind the government. Backed now by Moscow, Castro could defy Washington's attempt to destroy him.

His relations with the Soviet Union, however, were far from harmonious. He resented their attempts to place his regime under their thumb through some of his highly placed officials. In 1968 he jailed 35 of them. The Soviets retaliated by holding back oil deliveries to Cuba. Castro also displeased Moscow by insisting upon spreading revolution to other Latin American countries.

Castro's economic difficulties, and his dependence on Soviet aid, forced him to mend fences with the Russians. While he brooked no Soviet interference with Cuban sovereignty, he placated Moscow by going along with Soviet foreign policy. He supported the Russian invasion of Czechoslovakia in 1968 to put down a revolt. And in 1975 he sent Cuban forces to Angola to help a Soviet-backed African faction win a civil war.

But Cuba's police state remains basically Castro's personal one-man dictatorship. It is not a Communist regime in the sense that China and Russia are governed by a Communist party. As First Secretary of the party and Prime Minister, Castro is the supreme authority. The Cubans call his bold, blundering, colorful style of personal rule *Fidelismo*. They delight in his unpretentious, informal manner. At one rally in 1968 he even assumed the role of usher to direct the seating.

"We have some empty seats here," the Supreme Leader pointed out to his audience. "The comrades who are over there may move up to the platform, and the comrades who are in those rows can move up to the sides, some this way, others that way. Let us be close in all ways, eh?"

Confident of the affection in which his people hold him, Castro moves among them freely without bodyguards or any other form of protection, despite knowing of the CIA plots against his life. He often appears at small-town picnics or baseball games, where he buys ice-cream cones for the youngsters who flock around him. Immensely popular, he feels no need to plaster the country with photos or statues of himself. Castro is content to rest his claim to glory on what he has done for the Cuban people.

The Cuban masses know that Castro has made blunders, but they forgive him. They are convinced that he means well, works hard, tries his best, is personally honest, runs an honest government and has the interests of the poorest Cubans at heart.

Even if these perceptions were not valid, they would still be widespread because of the state-controlled media. As in any other police state, the press, radio and TV present only censored news, biased against the United States and other countries whose governments are at odds with Castro. He feels that this is justified inasmuch as he regards the portrayal of Cuba in the American and European press as equally prejudiced.

Castro's strong point has not been business management. When he eliminated 90% of private businesses in Cuba, making them state enterprises, he declared, "Gentlemen, we did not make a revolution here to establish the right to trade."

But as his close aide Che Guevara admitted, Castro and his revolutionists found running factories "a dull, depressing business." Production sagged. Consumer goods fell in short supply. Most of Cuba's managers, shopkeepers and professionals had fled to the United States. Few trained executives were left who knew how to run things well.

Castro so badly mismanaged the economy that he was forced to turn to Russian experts for advice and help in getting Cuba out of the mess. A new Cuban-Soviet trade treaty made Russian aid available to Cuba at the rate of $1 million a day.

Although democracy as such does not exist in Castro's Cuba,

workers' voices are heard through local Committees for the Defense of the Revolution (CDR). Most Cubans are members and air grievances at town hall meetings. These tend, however, to be primarily for the purpose of ventilating discontent harmlessly. A CDR chairman will often assure a complainant vaguely that "something is being done," while reminding workers at the meeting how much they have to be grateful for since Fidel made the Revolution for them.

The CDR also has the job of evaluating charges of loafing made against workers or officials under an Anti-Loafing Law Castro put through in April 1971. Absenteeism is a problem. Anyone judged a "lazy loafer" can be sentenced to a term of six months to two years of forced labor.

To encourage production, which is generally low, workers get a month's paid vacation. If they are hurt on the job, they are paid in full until their recovery. They are also fully covered by a social security program.

Before the Revolution, only half of Cuba's 6- to 12-year-olds were in school. Today almost every child is in a classroom. As a student in Cuba today you would find the schools much more regimented than our own, with lower-grade pupils wearing uniforms and drilling like soldiers. Where our school primers teach "A is for Apple," Cuba's teach "A is for Agrarian Reform" or "A is for Associated Press, the counterrevolutionary mouthpiece of the imperialist United States."

No matter how poor your parents or where they lived, you would have the same opportunity as any other Cuban child of getting the higher education you would need to become a doctor, engineer, lawyer, physicist or agronomist. You would not be taught to revere Fidel Castro the way Communist Chinese children are taught to revere Mao. But you would still be indoctrinated with Marxist-Leninist teachings, and taught to admire all revolutionary heroes who have overturned capitalist regimes.

At age 10 you would pick coffee. At 15, cutting or weeding sugar cane would become part of your education. Whether you aimed to become a manual or white-collar worker, or a professional of some kind, you would be taught that there are no class distinctions in revolutionary Cuba. Castro hopes eventually to have everybody working four hours and studying four hours, in universities built around farms and factories.

It has not been easy for him to get Cubans to accept the idea that manual labor is ennobling. In most Latin American countries it has long been looked down upon as degrading. Castro has sought to set an example by frequently going into the fields to work beside the cane cutters.

To force Cuban youth to do the manual labor Cuba needs, in 1973 Castro drafted them into a new paramilitary national labor organization. After graduation Cuban girls as well as boys are now required to spend three years in combined military and social service.

As a Cuban today you would enjoy the benefits of a welfare state —free health care, education, electricity, phone service, water, sports events and funerals. You would pay no income tax, and very little tax of any other kind. Rent would cost you only 10% or less of your salary.

There is still a small Cuban elite class. Top salaries of around $725 a month go to doctors, actors and top party leaders. That's a third more than the pay of a university professor. And *he* makes almost three times as much as a grade-school teacher or steelworker.

Millions of Cuba's poor who once lived in slums or wretched huts now have comfortable and adequate, if not luxurious, accommodations. There are also lots of day-care centers for mothers who work or study at schools or universities.

Although there has been a sizable increase in the number of doctors trained, medical care has presented a problem because of all the middle-class doctors who left after the Revolution, and the jump in Cuba's population. Nonetheless Cuba has the best health record of any Latin American country. All new doctors are required to spend two years in rural health centers after medical training. Cuba also has special schools for the blind, deaf and handicapped.

Food is still rationed, except for fish and beer. Before the Revolution most Cubans could not afford milk. Castro has built up a dairy industry which has turned today's Cubans into milk drinkers. Emphasis is laid upon supplying daily milk for children under age 7.

There is no conspicuous bureaucratic elite that flaunts its privileges by driving around in limousines, eating at expensive restaurants and vacationing abroad, as there was in the corrupt old Batista days. As much as possible, Castro tries to enforce equal treatment for all. A great deal of Cuban production depends upon the voluntary sharing of hard work. If volunteers saw a Cuban elite living in luxury, few would continue to sacrifice their spare time and effort to help build what they have been taught to believe is a classless society.

Cuba is a typical Left-wing police state in that it discourages religion and harnesses most cultural programs for propaganda purposes. Although there is freedom of worship in Cuba, the government seeks to attract youth away from the Catholic Church by arranging Sunday play and work programs.

A 1971 Cuban National Congress on Education and Culture resolved that culture must serve the state. "Art is a weapon of the Revolution," it declared. ". . . Our art and literature will be a valuable tool for the formation of our young people in the spirit of revolutionary morals."

The Castro regime has brought cultural programs to the Cuban masses in a way never before attempted. Three symphony orchestras tour the island, and many small towns sponsor government-assisted local orchestras. The countryside has also been opened up to ballet, theater, poetry recitals and traveling libraries. None of these cultural activities, however, permits any viewpoint that could be construed as antigovernment.

"There is serious mental starvation in Cuba—just about two books per capita, and mostly schoolbooks," complained one high-school teacher. "These kids can't imagine a real bookshop, thousands of books, Right-wing, Left-wing books, cramming out the shops."

The government puts pressure on people to attend civic meetings. Those who don't feel a chill of party disapproval. As in most Communist countries, there is a lack of privacy. Neighbors observe neighbors—how each lives, with whom each associates. Nonconformists are automatically suspect.

Nevertheless Castro's Revolution has brought about many changes welcomed by Cubans. People eat better. The literacy rate has increased dramatically. Black Cubans have been given equality. Gambling and prostitution have been wiped out along with graft. No more barefoot children beg in the streets. No more hungry jobless plead for work. Few police are necessary because Cuban cities have little crime or violence.

Many impressive innovations have also taken place in health care and education. Women, once an oppressed and neglected class, now make up half of all university and medical students. New schools, hospitals, housing developments and dairy farms also spotlight the brighter side of Castro's regime.

On the other hand, out of a 9-million population there are still an estimated 20,000 political prisoners in Castro's jails. And there are unproved allegations that torture has been used by overzealous jailors.

Cuba, in other words, is a complex police state with much that is both good and bad. "It makes no sense to think of Cuba in North American terms," writes Herbert Matthews in *Revolution in Cuba*; "to measure her with the yardsticks of Western liberal democracy; to expect Latin Cubans to feel and think like Anglo-Saxons and to want what we in the United States want."

The Revolution has to be accounted a success from the viewpoint of the Cuban masses. If Cuba today is drab, it is also free of the ugly garishness that marked the crime- and racket-ridden Batista regime. If the shops are depressing, the great majority of Cubans at least now have the bare essentials they need and a bit more. The people have accepted hardships, frustrations and disappointments because they approve of a revolutionary government that shares food evenly, doesn't discriminate, gives priority to schools and hospitals, and guarantees every Cuban a job.

Above all they admire Fidel Castro and trust him as their friend. "Fidel left a life full of food to go hungry in the Sierra," explained one Cuban youth. Most young men and women in Cuba have been trained in idealism to the point that they are ready to work hard, and die if necessary, to win Cuba's fight against poverty, disease and the American boycott. It is this determination that enables them to endure the dull, boring work of chopping sugar cane or running machines.

For these reasons, too, it does not bother most Cubans that Castro is running a one-man dictatorship, without elections or a parliament,

100

and with no opposition party or press allowed. As for Cuba's dependence on a foreign power, Castro points out that the Russians don't own an acre of Cuba, while under Batista the Americans owned enormous holdings.

In 1971 the Castro regime jailed Cuban poet Herberto Padilla for criticizing Cuba's lack of freedom. He subsequently "confessed" his sins. The confession was denounced by writers around the world, including Jean-Paul Sartre and Alberto Moravia, as obviously obtained by force or threat. Castro angrily attacked these noted critics as a "mafia of bourgeois intellectuals" and "pseudo-Leftists."

While there is no real criticism of Castro in the media, few Cubans hesitate to complain to him to his face. In one village he visited, a woman berated him for the low water pressure in her apartment. He sighed, "Here you have free electricity, a television set, and pay no rent—yet you complain about the water pressure!" She laughed.

Freedom to vote or read a free press, in Castro's view, is not nearly as important to people as the freedom to eat enough, to learn to read and write, to be taught a trade, to get a job, to be treated with dignity, and to have good medical care. Cubans who disagree and seek to leave Cuba are punished by losing their jobs and ration books. They are required to work in the fields, until their departure is arranged, "to grow the food they eat." Those who emigrate cannot take their property with them. Boys of military age cannot leave.

Like Lenin, Castro insists that when a final judgment is possible, history will absolve him for his Revolution.

3

In April 1941 Hitler's mechanized divisions thundered across the borders of Yugoslavia. Over 1,500 German bombers rained destruction on Belgrade, the capital, killing 20,000 civilians and wounding thousands more. The city was reduced to charred ruins. King Peter fled by plane to Greece, then London, where he established a government-in-exile.

Yugoslavia was a patchwork country made up of Croats, Slovenes, Serbians, Macedonians and Montenegrins. The country seethed with ethnic and religious hatreds. Hitler, who hated all Slavs, connived to have them destroy one another. Placing each region under a Yugoslav Fascist, he encouraged his puppets to massacre ethnic minorities within each region. Instead of uniting against the invaders of their country, the Yugoslavs fought each other bitterly in civil warfare.

Two guerrilla armies took to the hills to fight the Germans and their Yugoslav puppet forces. The Chetniks, led by Colonel Draža Mihajlović, were loyal to King Peter's government-in-exile. The anti-Fascist Partisans, led by Communist Josip Broz Tito, were the backbone of the resistance against the Germans. The Chetniks spent their chief efforts fighting the Partisans, rather than the Germans, considering Tito a greater threat to restoration of the monarchy after World War II.

Yugoslav peasants fully supported Tito. Even when his Partisan troops were hungry, they refused to touch a single grape in the vineyards which concealed them. "I've seen many an army in my day," one peasant landowner told a Partisan leader, "but never anyone like the Partisans. The people will be with you, and you will win for the simple reason that you are so honest!"

"Here we are among our own people," Tito told his ragged followers. "We must depend upon them for support, concealment, information, food and recruits. They must see for themselves that we Partisans are not the monsters the enemy tries to paint us, but decent neighbors who care about and respect them. We cannot, therefore, tolerate any violation of discipline."

Any Partisan who stole so much as a barley seed was executed formally in front of peasant observers.

Tito was at first an unabashed admirer of Stalin and the Soviet Union. He saw the Russian war against the Nazis as the significant world struggle against Fascism, which would decide the fate of every other country.

Stalin expressed appreciation to Tito. But he somehow always found excuses for not being able to airdrop desperately needed military supplies to the Partisans. Tito's enthusiasm for the Soviet Union gradually cooled.

As the war drew to a close, Stalin, for reasons of international politics, ordered Tito to accept a restoration of King Peter to the Yugoslav throne. Shocked, Tito refused. The Germans were driven out of Yugoslavia in a combined operation of Partisans and the Soviet Red Army. The Yugoslavs were angered when the Russians behaved as if they alone had liberated the country. Tito and Stalin also clashed over the undisciplined behavior of Soviet troops who were stationed in Belgrade.

They feuded again over Stalin's insistence that Tito must not try to industrialize the country. Stalin wanted Yugoslavia to remain a source of agricultural products and raw materials for the Soviet industrial economy. More and more, Tito grew to realize that Stalin's only interest in Yugoslavia was as a satellite to be used for Russia's needs, without regard for the needs and wishes of the Yugoslav people.

Tito was now both a war and revolutionary hero to all Yugoslavs. Although he was not an elected head of the nation, like Castro he had the overwhelming support of the masses, who idolized him. Defying Stalin's wishes, he promised Yugoslavs that no king would ever rule them again. A new Communist government would create a united Yugoslavia for the good of all, with no ethnic group subject to oppression by another.

"I have seven complicated problems," Tito said. "I have got *one* state that uses *two* alphabets, the Latin and the Slav; which speaks *three* languages, Serb, Croat and Slovenian-Macedonian; has *four* religions, Islam, Orthodox, Catholic and Judaism; *five* nationalities, Slovenes, Croats, Serbians, Montenegrins and Macedonians, *six* republics; and we have got *seven* neighbors!"

It was Tito who transformed this polyglot hodgepodge into a genuinely united nation. He kept the warring tribes, clans and sects from one another's throats by binding them together with national pride in being Yugoslavs first.

Standing up to Stalin, Tito declared that if his own experience contradicted the teachings of Karl Marx, he would obey the lessons of experience, not Marx. "I tell my associates that I want more fertilizers and more tractors," he said, "and less Socialist slogans."

Stalin was outraged by Tito's defiance and worried by the dangerous example he was setting for the leaders of other Communist nations. Tito had to be humbled and taught his place! For Tito the issue was the right of each Communist country to choose its own road to Socialism. Why should small Communist nations have to submit to the dictates of Moscow? Stalin had to be shown he couldn't bully the Yugoslavs around!

In 1948 Stalin "excommunicated" Yugoslavia from the Communist family of nations through the Cominform, the international Communist association dominated by Moscow. Tito was excoriated for "ambition, arrogance and conceit." The expulsion cut the Yugoslavs off from all Communist trade and aid until such time as Tito either repented and pleaded for forgiveness, or was thrown out by other Red leaders in Yugoslavia. When Tito wrote Stalin to protest, his letters were ignored and suppressed.

Tito ordered both the expulsion edict of the Cominform and his protest to Stalin published in the Yugoslav press. "Let the people judge for themselves who is right," Tito declared.

In a stunning and humiliating setback for Stalin, the Yugoslav Congress reflected popular opinion by voting complete support for Tito's position.

Yugoslavia's farms had been collectivized after the war, as in most Communist countries. Now Tito permitted any peasant who wanted to leave the collective farms and work on his own small holding to do so. He was lent machinery by cooperatives built on the Scandinavian model. Tito also decentralized the Yugoslav economy. Factories were directed by locally elected workers' councils, and to make sure they met the needs of consumers they were run on a profit basis.

The result was a participatory Communism quite different from the dictatorial Soviet model. Stalin furiously denounced "Titoism" as "revisionism." Ignoring him, Tito now felt free to experiment with other changes in the Communist system to make his regime even more flexible, successful and popular. He committed even worse heresy by turning to the West for military and economic aid. Playing his hand audaciously, he managed to persuade the United States, which was anxious to drive a wedge between the Soviet Union and other Communist countries, to reequip the Yugoslav army free of charge.

Tito's popularity soared. Yugoslavs admired his courage, independence and shrewdness. He became a symbol of independence from

Moscow envied by other people living under Communist police states in Europe.

In 1955 Khrushchev decided to go to Belgrade and apologize for the dead Stalin's long campaign of psychological, political and economic warfare against the Yugoslavs. This gesture, establishing Tito's right to build a different brand of Communism from the Russian model, increased Tito's prestige tremendously. In Eastern European countries pressure began to build for changes along the line the Yugoslavs had introduced—greater freedom of discussion, local control by workers' councils, the right of farmers to leave collectives, gearing the production of goods to needs of the marketplace.

Under Tito, Yugoslavia changed from a desperately poor, backward country to one where most people are satisfied with their lot. There are no more barefoot peasants. Much of the credit also goes to Tito's unique adaptation of the Western profit system, for the benefit of workers instead of capitalists. Local workers' councils now control factory production, hiring and firing, and the marketing of products. Although state-owned, Yugoslav enterprises compete with each other through advertising campaigns. The workers have an incentive to make quality products. If sales are good, they share the profits. If sales are poor, they earn less. Even if strikes were not illegal, few workers would support them.

"Why should I strike against myself?" one asked.

Although most Yugoslav workers are regimented in state-controlled industries, several hundred thousand are allowed to work for small firms employing up to five people apiece. In Tito's flexible economy, there is also room for small businessmen who are too fiercely independent to adjust well to becoming cogs in large state enterprises.

Tito's brand of Communism differs further from the Soviet pattern in granting freedom to travel abroad. As a Yugoslav worker, you would also be free to seek employment abroad, and to bring back reports of the much higher standard of living you found in the lands of the wicked capitalists.

Similarly, all of Yugoslavia is wide open to capitalistic tourists.

Tito is far less worried about what spies might find out about his regime than appreciative of tourist dollars.

Yugoslavia under Tito has become possibly the most progressive and pleasant Communist country in the world. It is even possible to discuss and contradict Tito's views in an uncensored press—up to a point. Until 1951 a large secret police force reached into every phase of daily existence, wielding the power to make arrests on the spot, spirit people off to jail and keep them locked up in unknown places for months.

Although Tito stopped their power to terrorize political opponents, Yugoslavia still remains a police state. Secret police still spy on the populace, reporting suspected threats to national security to the public prosecutor. If their suspicions seem justified, a court will order the secret police to conduct a full investigation.

Citizens who have seriously opposed Tito's policies have been arrested and jailed for "political crimes." Among them have been some of Tito's oldest comrades-in-arms like Milovan Djilas, who went to jail repeatedly for persisting in his view that the party bureaucracy ought to be replaced at regular intervals through democratic elections.

Whether Yugoslavia moves further toward liberalization or becomes a tighter, repressive dictatorship depends upon the Communist dictator who succeeds Tito. In either event, if the Yugoslav people are dissatisfied, they will not have the privilege of voting him out of office.

4

The people of Eastern Europe live under different types of Communist police states—dictated by Soviet arms. Most do not regard the Soviet Red Army as heroes for having rescued them during World War II from Hitler's Fascist-imposed regimes, but as plunderers who raped their countries, and instead of freeing them simply replaced Brownshirt dictatorships with Red ones.

Following World War II, Communists in each Eastern European country took over the government, backed by Soviet arms. Secret police arrested anti-Communists and put them in jail or used them

106

as slave labor. Russification campaigns made the study of Russian required in schools. Theaters were forced to show Soviet films, bookstores to feature Soviet books. Industry, transport, banking and foreign trade were nationalized and operated to suit Russian requirements. Against bitter opposition by farmers, farms were collectivized.

Stalin's death in 1953, followed by Khrushchev's speech denouncing him, stirred widespread unrest and hope for change among Eastern Europeans. Many demanded that their puppet dictators copy Tito's independent brand of Communism.

* * * * *

In 1953 the workers of East Germany took to the streets in mass demonstrations against the police state of dictator Walter Ulbricht. A flight of farmers to West Germany had caused food shortages. Shortages of consumer goods had also resulted from Ulbricht's order —made in Moscow—to concentrate on producing heavy industrial equipment, with a speedup of every worker's output.

Soviet troops joined East Germany's "people's police" in crushing the demonstrations. All meetings of more than three people were banned, and a 5 P.M. curfew was imposed. West German sources estimated that after the uprising 25,000 East Germans were sent to prison, with 62 executed as "militarists and Fascists."

Hundreds of thousands of skilled workers, engineers, doctors and other trained people fled to democratic West Germany through Berlin, a city located deep inside East Germany but divided in two between East and West German rule. In 1961 Ulbricht erected the Berlin Wall, a barrier up to 15 feet high topped with barbed wire, set in a zone of "death strips" guarded by armed watchtowers. The Wall sealed off and barricaded East Berlin from West Berlin. It was extended all along the East German border to stop the exodus of refugees to the West.

Desperate East Germans "voted with their feet," seeking to scale the Wall. Many were shot down by East German guards, and almost 3,000 were arrested.

By locking in its reluctant workers, the East German police state managed to produce a slow but steady economic improvement. But the regime, forced on the people by German Communists backed by Soviet power, was anything but popular among the people forced to live under it.

"You can hardly do anything without having to fill out a form," one citizen said in disgust. People with relatives in West Germany complained of the difficulty of getting passes to visit them. There was dissatisfaction with product quality—shoes, for example. "Way too hard," said one shoemaker. "The leather doesn't bend around that little bump by the big toe. Your feet get hard. That's why everybody walks so funny around here."

But East Germans approved of some of their government's innovations—particularly the social security system, pension plan, sickness and accident insurance, and other social services. The state paid bonuses for each child born. Pregnant workers received 14-week vacations. The state paid all funeral expenses. It was irksome to wait on long lines in order to see a clinic doctor, but the medical care was excellent.

The East German worker gradually grew reconciled to Communist rule. As his standard of living rose slowly to a level higher than that in other Eastern European countries—although much lower than that of West Germany—he grew less rebellious. He owned a TV set. His children received an excellent education. He took some pride in the reconstruction and expansion of industries which made East Germany first in industrial production among the satellites.

Dissatisfied East Germans are still escaping to the West, however. In 1975 another 5,000 fled by hiding in cars, defecting on tourist visas, using false passports, or being spirited out in sailboats, false-bottomed trucks and cargoes of fruit by professional "people smugglers."

*　*　*　*　*

The Communist rule imposed on Hungary by the USSR after World War II was harsh and arbitrary. The secret police (AVO) imprisoned many liberals, Socialists and even Communists suspected of being capitalist spies. They were beaten up, tortured and kept in prison for up to seven years. Some were killed. The innocence of most was later established after Stalinism had been discredited. They or their widows then received apologies and small sums of compensation.

Hungarian anger at Communist-imposed misrule exploded in October 1956. Thousands revolted. Party headquarters and bookstores were burned. Officials of the secret police were lynched. The Soviet Army was called in to put down the disorders.

Fighting against tanks, machine guns, artillery and planes, thousands of Hungarians were killed or wounded. János Kádár, a new, more liberal Hungarian premier installed by the Soviet Union, quickly introduced reforms. But Soviet soldiers continued to occupy the country. Many Hungarians fled abroad.

Under Kádár, Hungary began to tolerate cultural freedom as well as small private enterprise. Hungarians now also have the right to grumble openly without fear of the political police. Kádár and his government are loyal to Moscow, but nevertheless follow Yugoslavia in openly adopting some capitalistic practices.

Now voters are offered a choice of two candidates for each political office. Passports for travel abroad are easier to obtain, although an exit visa from the police is also required. Even more remarkable for a Soviet-controlled country, perhaps, was the permission granted parents of the young freedom fighters killed by Russian troops in the 1956 revolution to inscribe their tombstones: "Died a hero's death."

The Russian forces still occupying Hungary are referred to, when necessary, as "temporary." Hungarians are hostile toward them, but dare not demand that they go home. It is also taboo to criticize the Soviet Union. Hungarians are free to utter mild criticism of the Kádár regime, however—a safety valve for their discontent.

* * * * *

Soviet occupation also came hard to Czechoslovakia, which had enjoyed a Western-style democracy before invasion by Hitler in 1939 and occupation by the Red Army in 1945. The subsequent Communist puppet regime of Antonin Novotny was highly repressive. Over 130,000 Czechoslovakians were arrested for alleged crimes against the state. Some 50,000 were sentenced to over 10 years at hard labor.

One political prisoner described methods used to force him to confess guilt: "I was taken to some castle near Prague. I wore handcuffs and was blindfolded, my usual equipment over the years. . . . It was a cold February. So cold that the guards outside wore fur boots, coats and fur caps, and they were still freezing. I was wearing summer clothes. It was hot in the interrogators' rooms, the interrogators were in their shirt sleeves, and I was given an overcoat. I sweated all over. From the heat upstairs straight into the cold downstairs, again and again, day and night. Three officers shared the interrogation day and night, the insults, beatings, threats, the whole planned system of torture. The party sent you here, the party has made a decision about you, confess, confess!"

After Khrushchev's denunciation of Stalin in 1956, Novotny made concessions to Czech liberals. Some Stalinist officials were fired. Attacks on liberal journals and writers subsided. Some imprisoned church officials were freed. Western jazz, dancing and movies were tolerated.

But the hand of Communist repression remained heavy enough to provoke a protest demonstration by Czech university students in October 1967. Police squads broke up the demonstrators by hurling tear gas and beating them brutally. Outraged Czech workers protested by organizing job slowdowns.

According to Czech Writers' Union president Edward Goldstuecker, Novotny consulted Khrushchev about the trouble he was having with the Czechs. Khrushchev said, "You have to treat them like sparrows. If you had a sparrow in your hand, what would you do, Comrade Novotny?"

"I'd squeeze, Comrade, I'd squeeze," said Novotny.

"If you squeeze, you'll smother him. The sparrow dies. That creates one more scandal because the workers' republic needs its sparrows."

Novotny reconsidered. "Well then, I'd open my hand."

"Tsk! Tsk! The sparrow would only fly away. No . . . you keep the sparrow in one hand, not too tight, not too loose. With the other, you gently pull out one feather, then another, then all the feathers. When the sparrow is altogether naked, you can open your hand. He'll be so cold that he'll nestle down of his own accord."

But Novotny lacked the skill to tame the Czech sparrows. In 1968 he was forced out of office and replaced by liberal Alexander Dubcek as head of the Czech Communist party. Repudiating Novotny's

110

repressive regime, Dubcek promised new consideration for youth's demands, an end to censorship and the development of "more, and above all, deeper democratic forms."

Rejoicing, the Czech people staged huge demonstrations of support for Dubcek, who pledged to "make Socialism more attractive to the world." He instituted reforms that guided the Communist police in democratic directions. The Soviet Union grew concerned. Suppose this dangerous movement spread to the other satellite countries! The Red Army sent Eastern European troops into Czechoslovakia in May 1968 on what were represented to be "routine maneuvers" for the defense of the region.

Angry Czechs knew a threat when they saw one. Dubcek resisted all of Moscow's attempts to intimidate him into ending his attempts to democratize Communism. The Red Army then arrested almost all members of his government. The enraged Czech people organized a popular resistance. Now, big Soviet tanks rumbled across the border.

Dubcek was removed, replaced as party leader by Gustav Husak. Czechoslovakia once more became a police state in the iron Moscow mold. The books of all liberal writers were banned. Their homes were bugged, their phones tapped. Those who had won foreign recognition were interrogated for alleged involvement in a "conspiracy" against the state. Others were fired as editors and teachers, and forced to work as clerks and laborers. Some were jailed. Their foreign royalties earned abroad were confiscated. The homes of two dozen Czech writers were raided by police, who confiscated their manuscripts and notebooks. The Husak regime purged over 250,000 people from the Communist party and professional organizations.

"We suffer the fate of the silenced," leading Czech dramatist Pavel Kohout wrote to American playwright Arthur Miller, "and the Communist regime earns the shame of the one who has stilled our voices."

The bizarre logic that guides the policies of today's Czech police state is suggested by a recent Prague government edict. It declared, "Because Christmas Eve falls on a Thursday, the day has been designated a Saturday for work purposes. . . . Friday, December 25, has been designated a Sunday, with both factories and stores open all day. Monday, December 28, will be a Wednesday for work purposes. Wednesday, December 30, will be a business Friday. Saturday, January 2, will be a Sunday, and Sunday, January 3, will be a Monday."

If you live in a police state and the government says that Thursday is Saturday, Friday is Sunday, Monday is Wednesday, Wednesday is Friday, Saturday is Sunday, and Sunday is Monday, you had better believe it.

* * * * *

The Communist government of Bulgaria has sought to win the support of the nation's youth by giving them social and recreational advantages their parents had never known. Higher education is also available for the vast majority. Bulgarian youth generally support the system. But they also express frustration because they have been led to expect more than the government has been able to deliver, especially in terms of suitable jobs and housing.

"Why should I cherish illusions and dream of things in life that will probably never happen?" demanded one student. The government is disturbed because most of Bulgaria's youth admire all things Western tremendously.

Narodna Mladezh, the daily paper of the Communist youth organization, observed in pique, "They crowd around a car with foreign license plates, crane their necks in front of the bright windows of foreign legations. . . . They like nothing at home. According to them we have nothing, neither industry, nor literature, nor art, nor culture. While in the West . . . ! And they twist around to shrill sounds from tape recorders. . . . [They are] worshippers of all that is foreign."

The youth of Bulgaria, Czechoslovakia, Hungary, Rumania, East Germany and Poland all have one bond in common. They live under police states imposed upon their countries by the bayonets of the Soviet Army. Whatever economic advantages Communism may or may not have brought them, the price they pay is submission to a government they did not choose and cannot throw out. What freedoms they may enjoy from time to time, and in various degrees, are granted them as favors, not as rights guaranteed them in a constitution which cannot be set aside by a dictator.

112

VI

Variations on the Right

By 1936, just before World War II, there were 49 Fascist parties in 20 European countries. Even staunchly democratic England had its Fascist party under Sir Oswald Mosley. After his black-shirted followers paraded through London in 1937, starting street brawls with anti-Fascists, England felt compelled to ban the wearing of party uniforms by paramilitary groups.

This was a serious blow to the English Fascists. Flashy uniforms are part of the appeal of any Fascist movement, along with colorful banners, military songs, parades and daggers. Youth, in particular, is vulnerable to the dramatic trappings of violence, war and crisis.

Not only youth but the middle classes—from shopkeepers to civil servants and engineers—often support Fascist movements. They may approve of Fascist denunciations of the "bums" (poorer classes) who "have to be supported by taxes taken from the rest of us who work hard for our money." The middle classes also feel threatened by the demands of union labor, whom the Fascists usually denounce as "Communist controlled."

Because violence is the Fascist way of life, from street brawls to wars, political prisoners of a Fascist government are brutalized. During the Vietnam War, the Saigon police of South Vietnam, a police state, had a cynical rule for handling political prisoners: "If they are not guilty, beat them until they are."

Under Fascist rule, if you were suspected of being an enemy of the state, you might be hung upside down from an iron bar by your knees, burned with cigarettes, beaten with clubs, shocked by attached electric wires, or forced to swallow gallons of saltwater poured down your throat.

Amnesty International, the organization devoted to freeing political prisoners throughout the world, has worked to rescue over 13,000 known police-state victims, including some from Communist countries.

Torture is not unknown in the more brutal Communist police states, but it is more commonplace under Fascism. People who fight for Far Left causes tend to be more idealistic than adherents of the Far Right, observed Karl Hess, former chief speech writer for the ultraconservative Senator Barry Goldwater during the 1964 presidential campaign.

"To this I will swear," Hess wrote. "I do not personally know an active, persistent person on the Left who is in [it] for the money, the glory or the personal power. On the right I know scarcely anyone who was not."

2

Next to Adolf Hitler, the most famous Fascist in modern history was Benito Mussolini, dictator of Italy (1922–1943). Originally a Socialist, he broke with the antiwar party when the French government bribed him into advocating Italy's entrance into World War I by offering him his own newspaper.

"It is to you, youth of Italy," he wrote in it, "that I cry a terrifying and fascinating word: War!"

Fighting in the war himself, he returned home afterward to an Italy swept by unrest. The democratic government of Prime Minister Francesco Saverio Nitti, under King Vittorio Emanuele III, felt itself helpless to cope with severe problems that beset the country in the wake of the war. There were no jobs for demobilized workers. Soaring inflation had wiped out lifetime savings and had made it impossible for rural and urban workers to support their families. Militant labor unions called crippling strikes and seized industrial plants. There was also national indignation over the legions of war profiteers who were getting rich on black-market dealings.

When Nitti was voted out of office in June 1920, the new Prime

114

Minister tried to crack down on the profiteers, control inflation and raise taxes. Italian big business felt threatened and refused to cooperate. Labor, in turn, felt cheated out of its demands for social justice because of the government's timidity in dealing with the industrialists.

In effect, Italian democracy was crushed between two powerful millstones—labor and capital—both of which it was too weak to curb. Into this vacuum stepped Mussolini, who sought to build up a strong force of his own by organizing unemployed war veterans into the Fascist party. He pledged to restore "law and order" by means of violent attacks on Italy's Socialists, Communists, trade unions and consumer cooperatives, all of whom he labeled "red."

"However much one may deplore violence," he explained to his "squads of action," "it is clear that to make our ideas penetrate people's minds, we have to rap upon their unyielding skulls with cudgels. And who better fitted to carry out this gentle work of persuasion than the Fascist?"

Mussolini's street army wore black shirts, carried daggers and flags with a death's-head insignia, and saluted their commander with upraised arms and shouts of "Hail, *Duce* [Leader]!"

He used dramatic, emotional appeals to win the support of the lower middle classes—shopkeepers, middlemen, small landowners, some workers. He also made a secret deal with Italy's leading industrialists, bankers and landowners to destroy the country's labor unions, in return for financial support. Through the winter of 1920–1921 his Fascist squads attacked 300 Socialist strongholds, killing over 200 workers and wounding a thousand.

During their raids the police were always mysteriously absent. Outraged Socialist members of Parliament demanded that the government take action against the Fascists. But the King only congratulated Prime Minister Giovanni Giolitti on his "cleverness" in using the Fascists to destroy the "threat on the Left."

Mussolini's power grew rapidly. In May 1921 he and 33 of his followers were elected to Parliament.

That August the Socialists and other Left groups called a general strike to protest the government's unwillingness to stop violence by Blackshirt squads. The Fascists warned the government that unless it broke the strike within 48 hours, they would "demand full freedom of action, and substitute themselves for the State, which will once again have demonstrated its impotence."

Next day Fascist squads began serving as strikebreakers, delivering the mail and keeping trains and busses running. After some violent clashes between strikers and Fascists, the unions called off the strike. The Fascists claimed victory over both the "Reds" and the ineffectual government.

"Either the government must be handed over to us," Mussolini now warned, "or we shall seize it by marching on Rome!"

King Vittorio Emanuele, fearful of losing his throne, dissolved the government. He called upon Mussolini to form a new ministry. In October 1922 Mussolini led a march on Rome anyhow, for psychological effect, to give the impression of a violent seizure of power by his Fascist squads. There was no opposition. The Fascists made themselves the rulers of Italy with the full support of the country's ruling circles, whose interests they had secretly sworn to protect.

Those pledges were kept. The taxes of all who had helped the Fascist rise to power were promptly reduced. They were permitted to form business monopolies. At the same time these fattened corporate profits, the concentration of power gave the Fascists greater control over Italian workers and production.

Opposition parties were persecuted. Regional and local governments increasingly fell under Fascist control. Judges who refused to rule as the Fascists demanded were dismissed. Censorship was clamped on all universities and the press.

As in the days of ancient Rome, the Fascists diverted the masses with spectacles as a smokescreen for their moves to create a total police state. "The deathly stillness of the nation," observed Count Carlo Sforza, former Minister of Foreign Affairs, "is broken as often as possible by ceremonies, exhibitions, sporting events."

The Fascist squads gave free vent to their appetite for violent bullying. Personal enemies as well as political opponents were dragged from beds to be tortured, mutilated and shot. Their buildings were set afire and dynamited. The Fascist sense of humor was displayed in shaving off half a man's beard or mustache, forcing him

116

to swallow overdoses of castor oil, or "teaching him respect" with blows of a big club.

Although Mussolini aspired to increase his powers from those of a prime minister to those of an absolute dictator, he feared to move too precipitously because of powerful opposition in Parliament led by Giacomo Matteotti, popular head of the Socialist party. Matteotti created a sensation in Italy by accusing Mussolini, with proof, of secret deals with big industrialists to handcuff the unions; of assaults and murders; and of fraud at the ballot boxes. He promised an even more shocking revelation about the Fascists.

On June 10, 1924, the night before he was scheduled to make this new revelation, Matteotti was kidnapped by a Fascist squad and murdered. The assassination shocked all Italy. Legislators of the five opposition parties in Parliament walked out in a mass boycott of Mussolini's government. Wild street fighting broke out between Blackshirts and militant anti-Fascists.

Fearing overthrow of his regime, Mussolini turned power over to his most bloodthirsty aide, who instituted a reign of terror against all of Mussolini's enemies. The opposition collapsed. Mussolini now seized the opportunity he had been waiting for. On January 3, 1925, he dismissed Parliament, announcing he would henceforth rule as a dictator.

"If Fascism is an association of evildoers," he declared defiantly, "then I, myself, am the chief of these evildoers, and I boast of it! If Fascism has only been castor oil or a club, the blame is on me! If Fascism has been a criminal plot, if violence has resulted from it, the responsibility is all mine, because I deliberately created this atmosphere with my propaganda!"

Consolidating his control of the army, militia, press and courts, he set up secret political police and abolished all civil liberties. The slogan of his dictatorship was proclaimed: "Everything *in* the state—nothing *against* the state—nothing *outside* the state!" The state alone was supreme.

And Mussolini was the state.

If you had been a Catholic in Catholic Italy under him, you might have supported him at first because of his attacks on antichurch

Communists, Socialists and other Leftists. Mussolini introduced religious services into all state occasions. A crucifix was put up in every classroom. Leaders of the Freemasons, whom the Catholic Church considered enemies, were persecuted. Ironically, Mussolini himself was an atheist, but too shrewd not to appreciate the value of church support.

If you had been a worker, you might not have seen anything amiss in his transformation of labor unions into state-controlled "syndicates" without the power to strike. For one thing, his labor club movement provided workers and youth with sports, vacations, art exhibits, open-air movies and entertainment of all kinds.

"The people are ignorant children who must be taught, directed and looked after," Mussolini said privately. "Besides, if we don't control their leisure for them, they'll just use it to organize back-room plots against us!"

If you had been one of Italy's poor or jobless during the Depression, you would have been grateful to Mussolini for food relief distributed with the reminder, "Gift of the Duce."

As a radio listener you would have heard Mussolini's colorful, exciting speeches and the roaring responses of the crowds, creating an infectious enthusiasm for the Fascist cause. You would have been grateful for the entertainment provided by government stations— classical music, opera and drama as well as popular music. The news broadcasts you heard would have led you to admire Mussolini's accomplishments, such as getting the trains to run on time, and to deplore the terrible scandals going on in the democracies and Communist countries.

As a student you would have appreciated a free school lunch, and looked forward to going to a free summer camp. Here, in addition to enjoying sports, you would also have been taught the glories of Fascism, and how to march and use weapons.

Every high-school student had to take military instruction. But military discipline began much earlier. A third-grade textbook instructed: " 'Obey because you must obey.' Whoever looks for the reason for obedience will find it in these words of Mussolini."

As a youth in Mussolini's Italy, you would have been molded in the Fascist image by participating in mass organization activities several hours a week, and during summer outings.

As a member of a Fascist youth organization, you would have had to vow, "In the name of God and of Italy I swear to carry out the orders of the Duce and to serve with all my strength and, if necessary, with my blood, the Cause of the Fascist Revolution." Part of your oath would have required you to "correct . . . scold and silence" anyone who dared criticize the regime. And you would have sung, "To our enemies, a rock in the face—to our friends, all our heart!"

Under Mussolini the poverty of Italy's rural masses, especially in the south, grew worse than ever behind the facade of the soaring new white architecture in Rome and Naples. Even in the cities, one had only to leave the impressive main avenues by a block in any direction to find himself back in medieval slums. Few rural children went beyond the third grade of school. They were needed at home to help earn enough to eat.

Mussolini had come to power posing as an apostle of "law and order" at a time of violent labor struggles. Under his regime newspapers were forbidden to report crime news, giving the impression that his dictatorship had wiped out crime. In actuality, crimes caused by poverty rose steadily to a high level in 1937, when more thieves were arrested than ever before in Italian history.

If you had been dissatisfied with your lot under Fascism, you would not have been allowed to strike, organize a demonstration or even criticize the government, under penalty of imprisonment. The lack of dissent in the controlled press was cited by Mussolini's propaganda bureau as proof of general contentment with the Duce's policies.

In a few instances Italians became desperate enough to defy the police by staging demonstrations against hunger, low pay, wage cuts and job layoffs. To put food on the table, some families had to send children out to stone pigeons.

When Mussolini felt compelled to ally Italy with Nazi Germany in 1936, most Italians strongly disapproved. Neither anti-Semitic nor pro-German, they resented being made the tail to Hitler's kite. After 1939 Fascism became increasingly unpopular as Italy was dragged into World War II against Britain, France, the United States and the Soviet Union.

An Italian resistance movement sprang up. Factory workers struck. Housewives demonstrated against food shortages. Underground anti-Fascist fighters assassinated German and Italian officials and sabotaged war convoys. Mass arrests and deportation of striking workers to Germany failed to halt the unrest that swept the nation as Allied troops invaded Italy in 1943.

The armed resistance restored self-respect to the Italian people, absolving them of guilt and blame for the acts of the now-discredited Mussolini regime. The Fascist Grand Council denounced his bad leadership, and the King ordered his arrest and imprisonment. The Italian people staged wild celebrations as Marshal Pietro Badoglio replaced the police state with a democratic government that switched sides in the war.

Why had Mussolini risen to power in the first place?

A primary reason was the helplessness of Italy's democratic government after World War I to cope with the unemployment and inflation that had provoked widespread discontent and strikes. The government had viewed the "threat from the Left" as the chief peril. It had imagined that by giving Mussolini's Fascist street bullies a free hand to attack workers and break strikes, law and order could be restored.

Instead, Mussolini's march on Rome had indicated his contempt for legal processes. He had taken power legally at the invitation of the King, with the apparent consent of most Italians. They did not, however, anticipate yielding to him dictatorial powers.

Democracy fell in Italy basically because of the fatal mistake of the government in believing that by crushing the Left, even at the expense of strengthening the Right, it was protecting the nation's democratic institutions.

3

In 1931 Spain's King Alfonso, under whom an oppressive military dictatorship had wielded power, was driven from the throne. Popular elections gave Spain a democratic government made up of a coalition of moderate Republicans and Socialists, which became known as the Loyalist regime. One of its first acts was to pass new laws compelling separation of church and state, which weakened the power of the Spanish Catholic Church.

Spain's traditionalist military revolted in July 1936 "against the advance of Communism and anarchy." They were supported by monarchists, Right-wing groups, the Church, big landowners and bankers. General Francisco Franco emerged as head of the rebellion. He led an army of Moorish troops and Spanish Legionnaires, aided by 50,000 Italian "volunteers," tanks and heavy artillery supplied by Hitler, and bomber squadrons from both Fascist nations.

Franco told the Spanish people that his rebellion was a crusade on behalf of God and civilization against atheistic Communism. His real aims, however, had been stated in the program his Falange party propounded before unleashing civil war:

"Our State will be a totalitarian instrument in the service of National integrity. . . . No one shall take part in it through any political party. The system of political parties will be implacably abolished. . . . [Our] methods are preferably direct, ardent and combative. Life is a battle, and must be lived with a spirit alight with service and sacrifice."

Supporting the elected Loyalist government were Spain's Socialist and Communist parties, plus intellectuals, students, faculties, liberals, anarchists, republicans, anticlericals, and most workers and peasants. They were reinforced by a volunteer International Brigade of anti-Fascists from all over the world.

The volunteers saw the struggle in Spain as the opening battle of a world war for Fascism by Hitler and Mussolini. Some volunteers were German anti-Fascists whose teeth had been broken and whose fingertips had been crushed by Gestapo torture. Others included Communists, Yugoslav freedom fighters who later followed Tito, and Americans who made up the Abraham Lincoln Brigade.

Martha Gellhorn, an American correspondent covering the war in Spain, called the civil war "in its simplest and probably truest terms a war between the rich and the poor. Power was on the side of the rich from the first day. The Spanish poor had nothing except a fierce and stubborn loyalty to their Republic which they had won in honest elections and were determined to keep."

But passions were fierce on both sides, and each side was guilty of wartime atrocities. Anticlerical extremists in the Loyalist forces murdered thousands of priests, bishops and nuns, and burned hundreds of churches and convents. The head of the Associated Press in Spain reported that Franco's forces executed five times that many people by firing squad, and that his postwar executions ran to a staggering half million Loyalists.

In April 1937 on a market day in the pro-Loyalist Basque town of Guernica, Fascist bombers dropped explosives on the marketplace. Peasants were machine-gunned as they fled to the hills. Franco then ordered firebombs dropped on the city, turning it into a blast furnace.

This atrocity in bombing an open city was immortalized by the famous artist Pablo Picasso in the masterpiece known as the *Guernica* mural.

The Loyalist government received a small amount of aid from the Soviet Union and Mexico. The Western democracies refused to help, agreeing on a policy of "nonintervention" that "quarantined" the embattled nation by an embargo, making it difficult to get supplies to the Loyalists. Franco, meanwhile, continued to receive everything he needed from Germany and Italy, who used Spain as a testing ground for their new weapons.

The Spanish people fought stubbornly for three years, holding out longest in Madrid. Their government finally fell in March 1939, starved of arms, food, fuel and medicine, after 700,000 Spaniards had died in battle.

Taking over the country, Franco lost no time in turning it into a police state. No opposition movement or rival political party was permitted. Every opposition leader was jailed. Universities were destroyed as centers of intellectual ferment by placing them under police observation and control. Teachers were reduced to starvation wages. Strikes were outlawed.

Franco's parliament, the Cortes, was a burlesque of democracy. Two thirds of its members were appointed by Franco, the rest by Falangist organizations. Franco's Council of State decided which laws the Cortes was allowed to consider.

Total censorship was imposed on all newspapers, magazines and radio stations. Protestant and Jewish publications were banned. Any journalist or editor responsible for an item that displeased the government was fired instantly. Textbooks used in the public schools explained censorship to children:

> *What does "freedom of the press" mean?*
>
> *The right to print and publish without censorship all kinds of opinions, no matter how absurd and corrupt they may be.*
>
> *Should the Government repress this freedom by means of previous censorship?*
>
> *[Obviously] yes . . . it must prevent the deception, calumny and corruption of its subjects which are harmful to the common good.*
>
> *Are there other pernicious freedoms?*
>
> *Yes, sir; freedom to teach, freedom to make propaganda and to hold meetings.*
>
> *Why are these freedoms pernicious?*
>
> *Because they are used for teaching error, spreading vice and plotting against the Church. . . .*
>
> *Does he who subscribes to liberal papers sin gravely? Yes, sir. . . .*
>
> *What rules can you give for recognizing liberal papers? . . .*
>
> *If they stand for freedom of conscience, freedom of worship, freedom of the press or any one of the other liberal errors.*

If you were a worker in postwar Fascist Spain under Franco, even by 1959 you would have earned an average annual income of only $400. The minimum wage was 70¢ a day, agricultural wages far less. Low pay was slightly compensated for by a system of social insurance, with a family allowance for each child. But many workers were forced to hold two jobs in order to provide for their families. Few could afford to buy their children enough milk to drink. At the same time 202 big corporations were exempted from paying taxes on their profits—"in the national interest," Franco explained.

If you were a woman, your chance of holding a good job would have been far less than a man's. There was twice as much illiteracy among women; few went beyond high school. In 1957–1958 there were five times as many men as women in Spain's universities. Like Hitler and Mussolini, Franco felt that a woman's place was in the kitchen, bedroom and nursery. He offered wedding subsidies to brides who agreed to stay home and not seek a job.

Even after almost a quarter century of rule, Franco failed to win the hearts and minds of the Spanish people.

"Probably, all in all, something between 80 and 90% of the people as a whole oppose Franco," journalist John Gunther observed in 1961, "but they have no means of displacing him." There was no mechanism for an election and the civil war had left deep scars upon most Spaniards, who had no heart for another savage bloodletting.

"Hitler had the German youth with him, and Mussolini the Italian youth," noted Prime Minister Jawaharlal Nehru of India. "Franco has not succeeded in attracting the Spanish youth. That fact is very promising and very important." Most of Spain's young people became Leftist and militant, demanding an end to the reign of Spanish Fascism.

The growing opposition to Franco in the 1970's included a separatist movement in the Basque area known as the ETA, a radical underground in Barcelona and clandestine labor unions who defied the laws against strikes. Franco grew increasingly helpless to enforce the antistrike laws because it was impossible to expel or arrest hundreds of thousands of workers who went out on strike. In 1974 alone there were over 2,000 strikes, affecting over a thousand companies and idling 700,000 workers.

The ETA and some Marxist organizations began to fight Franco with terrorism. Bombs blew up police stations and killed Franco's officials. Franco responded with counterterror. His police swept up thousands of "suspects," grilling them by torture. Military tribunals sentenced ten accused terrorists to death. Their impending executions stirred indignant protest demonstrations all over the world; Spanish embassies were burned in 3 European capitals, and 15 European governments recalled their ambassadors from Madrid.

When some 200,000 Basques walked out of their factories and classrooms to protest the hundreds of political prisoners, most of them Basques, being held in Spanish jails, police opened fire on their demonstrations.

Then, shaken by the world outcry against his police state, Franco organized a mass demonstration of 200,000 of his supporters in Madrid. They roared approval of him and their defiance of the rest of Europe. But the orchestrated cheers were for an aging dictator whose power was being forced from his hands by approaching death.

As Franco lay dying, his bureaucrats took measures against the possibility of a new Leftist revolution. The dictator's opponents were beaten up and warned to get out of the country within 24 hours after his death. This violence was intended to remind Franco's heir apparent, Prince Juan Carlos, that even with Franco dead his officials intended to perpetuate his police state.

Sworn in as King of Spain after Franco's death in late 1975, Juan Carlos expressed "respect and gratitude" to the late dictator and swore allegiance to the principles of the Fascist National Movement. But he was aware of the great desire of the Spanish people for change and an end to the police state. He sought to go as far as the Fascist bureaucracy would let him to persuade Spaniards he was liberalizing the regime.

Stormy demonstrations by Leftists made it clear to the anxious new King that they would not be satisfied with just a milder form of Francoism. Correspondent Martha Gellhorn, revisiting Spain after Franco's death, reported, "No one knows how many people are arrested by the police, beaten, not charged, and dismissed." Estimating that some 100,000 were awaiting trial and sentencing, she noted, "The police are the absolute power of oppression and above the law."

Carlos promised to hold free parliamentary elections and to grant amnesty to all political prisoners. But Franco's Prime Minister decreed that representative democracy would not be allowed for at least another two years. Nor would political prisoners be freed before then.

The King managed to oust the old Prime Minister half a year later, replacing him with a political moderate, Adolfo Suárez, who slowly began to dismantle the dictatorial institutions of Franco Spain. Less than a year after Franco's death, under Suárez's leadership, the largely appointed Parliament left behind by Franco approved general elections for 1977, and voted itself out of existence. With the first free elections scheduled since those held by the Loyalist government in 1936, Spain apparently was returning to the ranks of the democracies.

Spain might never have become a police state in the first place if the Western powers had not turned their backs on the Loyalist government in 1936. Their refusal of aid made it certain that Franco, with help from Hitler and Mussolini, would win the civil war against the elected regime. Though the Spanish people as a whole had supported the Loyalists, they were helpless to stop the powerful military juggernaut.

4

Most Latin American police states are controlled by a powerful handful of wealthy families and defended by the army and a police apparatus, while the masses live in wretched squalor. Dom Helder Camara, Archbishop of Pernambuco, Brazil, had some observations about those who wield such power:

"Unfortunately the rich in Latin America talk too much about reform and label as Communists all those who would enforce it. This is easy to understand: The rich in Latin America go on holding 80% of the land on the continent. Often they control parliament and have the intensity of their idealism and hope in the future gauged by the bank deposits kept in their names in the United States and Europe."

The police state in Uruguay represents a marriage of convenience between powerful business interests and the military. Political parties, labor unions and a free press are banned. "Any criticism or opposition to the armed forces," reports Amnesty International, "is labeled as subversion and carries with it arbitrary arrest without legal safeguards and with maltreatment, torture and heavy prison sentences."

* * * * *

In Chile, two American companies—the International Telephone and Telegraph Corporation (ITT) and Anaconda Copper—were heavily invested. They grew alarmed in 1970 when it seemed likely that Salvador Allende Gossens, a declared Marxist candidate, might win the Chilean elections and seek to transform the country into a Socialist state. ITT officials met with officials of the American CIA's Clandestine Services branch to discuss ways of sabotaging Allende's election campaign, and to prevent him from taking office if he won. ITT offered $1 million to the CIA to finance these operations. The money was refused, but the CIA pursued this objective on its own.

Secretary of State Henry Kissinger, presiding over White House meetings of the top-secret "40 Committee" that guided American foreign policy, deliberated over how to stop Allende. Kissinger was determined that Chile must not have a Marxist president even if the people elected him. According to *Newsweek*, he told the 40 Committee, "I don't see why we should stand by and watch a country go Communist due to the irresponsibility of its own people."

When Allende was elected, ITT representatives in Chile sent a secret memo to their home office reporting that the American Ambassador had received "the green light to move in the name of President Nixon . . . to keep Allende from taking power." The Chilean army "has been assured full material and financial assistance by the U.S. military establishment," and ITT had "pledged support" to the anti-Allende forces.

When Allende was sworn in as President, the Nixon Administration sabotaged his regime by cutting off economic assistance and blocking credit and loans from international organizations. Military aid to Chile's Right-wing generals and admirals, however, was increased until it reached levels higher than those of any other country in Latin America.

One of Allende's first acts was to provide free milk for every child in Chile. "If I were to die tomorrow," he declared, "no one in Chile would ever dare to abolish the system."

But the American economic blockade made other such spending programs impossible by strangling Chilean industry, transportation and communications. The U.S.-controlled Agency for International Development funneled huge amounts of cash to Chilean centers of anti-Allende opposition. So did the CIA, which planted anti-Allende propaganda in the Chilean press and manipulated strikes and demonstrations against him.

Finally, in September 1973, Chile's army staged a coup. Attacking the Presidential Palace, the military overthrew the democratic Marxist government and murdered Allende. The American government quickly protested that it had had nothing to do with the coup or the assassination of Chile's president.

Establishing martial law, Chile's new junta explained that their coup had been necessary to "save the nation" from "the Marxist cancer." They promised a government of national reconciliation and economic reconstruction. No one, pledged General Augusto Pinochet Ugarte, would be persecuted for his or her ideas. The army was "above politics," and would be guided in its actions only by "the national interest."

The new police state, supported by the United States, suspended the nation's constitution, shut down its congress, silenced or censored the press, and banned all political parties and all trade-union activity.

Reversing Chile's economic direction, the new military junta let the price of necessities soar 2,000% in two years—the world's fastest inflation rate. Unemployment rose by 20% as many small businessmen went bankrupt. Many workers could no longer afford bus fares to their jobs. Many families were reduced to bread and tea; schoolchildren began fainting from hunger; and beggars began to appear on the streets. "Malnutrition," reported *The New York Times*, "is the rule in Santiago shantytowns." On the other hand, real-estate speculators, finance companies, the military and other privileged classes in Chile prospered.

Catholic Church sources in Chile estimated that 100,000 Chileans were being held in detention camps as political prisoners, many suffering torture. The new adviser to Chile's dreaded secret police, the DINA, was Walter Rauff, an ex-Nazi colonel who had been second in command of Hitler's program for the extermination of European Jewry.

The international outcry against Chile's brutal police state became so great that even though President Gerald Ford remained silent, in February 1976 the U.S. Congress cut off all military aid to the Chilean junta. Senator Hubert Humphrey described it scathingly as "a group of generals who act like thugs."

Even before taking office in 1977, the new American President, Jimmy Carter, warned the Chilean junta that total U.S. aid would be cut off from regimes that trample on human rights. Next day the junta hastily announced the release of almost 300 political prisoners, trying to give the impression that political repression was a thing of the past in Chile. But nothing was said about over 700 other political prisoners sentenced or on trial, according to Amnesty International, nor 1,500 more who had simply "disappeared."

5

In 1961 when João Belchior Marques Goulart was elected president of Brazil, there was trepidation among the country's wealthy conservative class. Goulart was a reformist determined to better the lives of the impoverished masses. The army and big business conspired to reduce his powers by getting the Brazilian Congress to pass a constitutional amendment to this effect.

Goulart won a plebiscite restoring the president's powers, but runaway inflation provoked a financial crisis. The unions pressed for higher wages and called a series of crippling strikes. Goulart, a weak leader who felt helpless to cope with the situation, appointed Left-wing leaders to critical posts in the government. Under their guidance he sought to pacify labor, introduce rent control, extend the vote to illiterates, recognize the Communist party, nationalize Brazilian-owned oil companies and initiate land reform.

In March 1964 the armed forces, supported by Brazilian business interests, big landowners and most of the middle class, overthrew the Goulart democracy.

General Humberto Castelo Branco promised "a government of law and an early return to democracy." Scheduling new elections, he disqualified members of the Goulart faction and other "undesirables" from opposing him. Having thus assured his victory, Castelo Branco was shocked when his regime still lost in five out of the eleven contested states of Brazil. He and other officers of the junta then abolished all political parties. The results of elections where they had lost were nullified. Direct elections were abolished. So much for the early return to democracy. There has since been a succession of heads of state, none of them elected by the people.

Like most police states, the Brazilian regime persecutes all opponents, using torture and other forms of official terror. When revolutionists organized guerrilla bases to overthrow the dictatorship, they were wiped out by Brazilian troops backed by American-supplied bomber and fighter planes.

The People's Revolutionary Vanguard (VPR) struck back in 1971 by kidnapping Western diplomats. The hostages were held until the regime agreed to release political prisoners, give wage increases and permit publication of a manifesto calling upon the workers of Brazil to revolt. Their manifesto charged the regime with having the highest child death rate in the world, with permitting glaring social injustices including slavery, with exploiting the poor and with turning the country over to foreign capital to exploit.

Philip Agee, who worked for the CIA for twelve years, observed, "Repression in Brazil even includes cases of the torture of children, before their parents' eyes, in order to force the parents to give information. This is what the CIA, police assistance, military training and economic aid programs have brought to the Brazilian people."

The Brazilian government responded to the revolutionary movement with mass arrests, indiscriminate torture of all who *might* have information, and the organization of off-duty police into "death squads" to kill critics of the regime. All Brazilian householders were instructed to spy on their neighbors and report any suspicious behavior or overheard comments.

The government's use of troops and mass arrests succeeded in crippling the VPR.

6

When the Nazis were driven out of Greece at the end of 1944, Communist resistance forces sought to take power. They were defeated by Greek Royalist and British troops. Almost thirty years of repressive Right-wing rule followed. Finally, in 1964, George Papandreou, leader of the moderate Center Union Party, won election as Premier.

King Constantine, the army and Right-wing parties were alienated by the liberal policies of Papandreou and his son and aide, Andreas, who viewed the Right as the enemy of Greek democracy. Andreas Papandreou also felt the American embassy in Athens was in collusion with parties of the Right.

Premier Papandreou introduced many needed reforms. All education became free, compulsory to the first year of high school. Textbooks were modernized, teacher training improved, and free school meals provided to children in rural areas. The Right-wing opposition denounced Papandreou as a Communist. But the Greek people reelected him with an increased majority.

Continuing his reforms, he cut back the power of the army and the Crown, while extending the rights of the people. The Left was allowed to publish newspapers, hold meetings and organize demonstrations. Police certificates of "civic reliability," issued only to those who voted for Right-wing candidates, were no longer required to get government jobs. Greeks were once again free to speak their minds, without fear of arrest if their views displeased government officials.

A group of outraged Army colonels, led by Colonel George Papadopoulos, whipped up a propaganda campaign against Papandreou in the Right-wing press. They charged that Greek democracy was breaking down, and that the country was endangered by a Communist plot to seize power through subverting the army. The chief plotter, accused the colonels, was the son of the Premier, Andreas Papandreou.

King Constantine held worried consultations with the army general staff and the U.S. Embassy. He then forced the resignation of Premier Papandreou, appointing a conservative politician in his place. The Greek people rallied to support the ousted Premier and his son. Huge street demonstrations, booing the King, were broken up by police violence.

The Center Union and the Left protested that the King had violated the Greek Constitution by arbitrarily dismissing the people's elected representative.

On Friday, April 21, 1967, if you had been a Greek citizen, you would have gone to bed under a democracy and awakened next morning under a dictatorship. Papadopoulos and the Greek colonels took the King and all political parties by surprise by seizing power with a few army units.

Morning news broadcasts half an hour later revealed the coup. Citizens were ordered not to leave their homes on pain of being shot. The King, said the announcer, had asked the army to intervene in order to prevent a great danger to the nation that had arisen during the night.

Those who tried to call a friend, relative or neighbor found their phones dead. Not daring to go out, they simply waited for further instructions. Later news informed them that most members of the government and many politicians of the opposition had been arrested. The King, it was stated, had signed a proclamation of martial law giving the new military junta power to rule by decree. Finally, citizens were told to report to work as usual or go about weekend shopping.

The colonels had lied to the Greek people about authorization of their coup by the King. Nor had he signed their decree of martial law. But the Greek public had no way of knowing that during the crucial hours when the putsch took place. Only after the coup was a *fait accompli* did the King reluctantly sign the decree. Instead of refusing, and calling upon the Greek people and the whole army to resist, he yielded to the plotters and let Greece become a police state.

Using a large secret-police force, the colonels inaugurated a harsh dictatorship. Six thousand men and women were dragged from their beds and herded into prisons and concentration camps. All political parties were dissolved. Every newspaper was compelled to print the same propaganda praising the junta for saving Greece from Communism. No uncensored news was permitted to appear. Popular books and music unacceptable to the ultraconservative colonels were banned.

No more than five persons were allowed to meet together in public or private without permission. Citizens could be arrested without warrant and detained indefinitely without trial. Special courts-martial could try anybody for anything, without regard to laws. Strikers or critics of the government received five-year jail terms. All children, teachers and civil servants were compelled to attend church on Sundays.

The junta took control of every aspect of Greek life by purging all areas of government, from education to the courts and armed forces. Its own men were placed in key posts.

Thirty of Greece's most distinguished judges were thrown out overnight, deprived even of the right to practice law. This hint was not lost on other Greek judges. They hastened to find guilty and sentence severely all defendants prosecuted by the state, no matter how trumped up the charges. Lawyers who undertook to defend such accused persons were threatened with arrest themselves for "disloyalty."

Friends and supporters of the junta were rewarded by a reduction and cancellation of taxes for wealthy industrialists, landowners, bankers and shipping magnates. Doubling the Greek budget for propaganda, the colonels also quadrupled expenditures for government-sponsored soccer as a diversionary spectacle to distract the public, and for those youth organizations that lined up behind the junta. Military officers were given large raises, free travel, free loans and special discount privileges in buying merchandise.

The junta also sought to win the support of various civilian groups. Debts of the larger farmers were canceled. Social security was extended to peasants. Low-cost housing was begun for workers. University students were issued free textbooks. For the most part, however, the colonels' program for the country was explained succinctly by Papadopoulos in December 1969. "The Greek people," he said, "must eat less, work more and demand less."

Civil servants were forced to work overtime at no extra pay. Hundreds of active trade unionists were arrested and sent to concentration camps, and 158 unions were outlawed.

The heavy hand of the dictatorship drove most of Greece's foremost writers, artists, actors and directors either to jail or self-imposed exile abroad. Intellectuals who remained were suspected of plotting against the government, even when they met just to discuss literature. They were often arrested and detained for weeks in a war of nerves waged by the secret police.

Greeks suspected of resistance were routinely tortured. Reports about the torture dungeons were allowed to circulate freely, in order to frighten off all Greeks tempted to join the underground.

Popular opposition to the dictatorship persisted. In November 1968, at the funeral of George Papandreou, a Greek crowd of almost half a million people attended in defiance of martial law. "Long live freedom!" they cried. "We want elections!" About 40 people were seized and jailed.

Papadopoulos now emerged from the junta to rule as sole dictator. He required up to 300 policemen to protect him when he moved between his home and office. Slashing the budget for education, he increased expenditures for the military until they accounted for half the national budget. Also increased were the budgets for networks of informers engaged in spying upon and intimidating the regime's opponents outside Greece.

In November 1973 Greek workers and students rioted against Papadopoulos. Unable to restore order, he was replaced by a Right-wing rival, Colonel Demetrius Ioannides, Commander of the Military Police. But the junta collapsed when it tried to annex the island of Cyprus, only to have Turkey invade Cyprus and seize former Greek territory.

Former Premier Constantine Karamanlis was recalled from exile as head of the New Democratic Party. Freeing all political prisoners, he held honest elections in November 1974. The New Democrats won a majority in Parliament. In a referendum one year later, Greeks rejected restoration of the monarchy and voted to make Greece a parliamentary republic.

Most Greeks blamed the United States for having given massive financial and military support to the junta. "We helped keep it in power," acknowledged Senator Thomas Eagleton.

But the important thing for the Greek people was that at last the land that had given the institution of democracy to the world had, after a nightmare experience under dictatorship, once more returned to the free and open society that was its great heritage.

7

From 1828 until 1947 India was a colony of the British Empire, ruled by harsh suppression of all political opposition and agitation. In 1930 Mahatma Gandhi, aided by Jawaharlal Nehru, began waging a campaign of civil disobedience to win freedom and democracy for India. Jailed repeatedly for their political opposition, the martyrs won huge popular support.

Finally, in August 1947, India was granted independence as a self-governing member of the British Commonwealth. It became a democratic republic in January 1950. As such it offered a striking contrast to the police states of the other giants in Asia, China and the Soviet Union.

Nehru governed India as Prime Minister until 1964. Two years later his daughter, Mrs. Indira Gandhi (no relation to Mahatma Gandhi), became Prime Minister. But in June 1975 an Indian court ruled that she had won election to Parliament in her 1971 campaign illegally. Political opponents began a campaign of demonstrations and strikes to compel her to step down.

Declaring a national emergency, Mrs. Gandhi responded by arresting over 100,000 of her opponents and imposing strict press censorship. These harsh measures revoking Indian democracy seemed ironic, decreed by the daughter of an Indian patriot who had been jailed himself so many times for political opposition. Fresh demonstrations erupted against her. Swinging lead-tipped canes, police broke them up, making mass arrests. In a few cities demonstrators were even fired upon.

Mrs. Gandhi imposed a virtual blackout of all news reports of demonstrations and arrests. Five New Delhi newspapers were shut down, and some editors jailed. Papers were not permitted to print any criticism of Mrs. Gandhi or her government, nor mention that the press was being censored.

When foreign correspondents filed stories reporting what was going on, their papers and magazines were banned in India. The government demanded that all foreign correspondents sign a pledge to comply with censorship rules. The U.S. embassy pressured American reporters to sign. Some TV correspondents who did filed phony dispatches with government censors, got okays, then phoned or airlifted their real stories secretly.

"In ten years of covering the world from Franco's Spain to Mao's China," *Newsweek*'s Loren Jenkins cabled home, "I have never encountered such stringent and all-encompassing censorship." He was expelled for refusing to sign the pledge, along with two recalcitrant London correspondents.

Mrs. Gandhi banned extremist parties of the Left and Right. To permit police to jail anyone for up to two years without explanation, the existing right of habeas corpus was suspended. Mrs. Gandhi also banned strikes and froze wages, in a bid for the support of India's businessmen.

The world was shocked that the model Indian democracy had, in so short a time, been transformed into a police state. Especially by the arbitrary decrees of a Prime Minister everyone assumed shared the ideals of her famous father. Despite some concessions to the poor, her regime operated like a Right-wing dictatorship.

"The most remarkable thing about Mrs. Indira Gandhi's swift seizure of power and effective suspension of democracy in India is how easily it was accomplished," observed Tom Wicker in *The New York Times*. "It also seems to have been widely accepted, if first reports are borne out, although it had generally been assumed that Indian democratic traditions were strong and deep. . . . The defenders of Mrs. Gandhi's action delude themselves if they assert that she took it to save Indian democracy. Instead, she took advantage of its weakness and may well have destroyed it."

One reason most Indians accepted Mrs. Gandhi's police state is that her severe censorship kept them from knowing the full truth about it. Instead, they were propagandized with new reform decrees she hastily introduced to win popular support—measures to control prices, crack down on hoarding shopkeepers, protect small farmers from debt collections, distribute a little surplus land among the landless and reduce income taxes for the lower middle class.

Millions who knew what was happening began behaving as people traditionally do in a police state. Apprehensive that their phones were bugged, they were guarded in their phone conversations with friends. Indians meeting for lunch could be observed glancing anxiously over their shoulders, in case police spies might be eavesdropping. Conversation halted at the approach of a waiter or stranger.

In Madras, however, 100,000 people packed the beaches along the Bay of Bengal to take a mass oath: "We will not hesitate to take prompt steps to prevent the downfall of democracy in India. . . . Long live democracy, the people's rule!" From the underground, where many opposition leaders had fled, came mimeographed appeals for revolution. Accusing Mrs. Gandhi of being power mad, the leaflets warned, "A Fascist dictatorship has been clamped on our land." One underground journalist declared, "We cannot do much right now other than stay a step ahead of the police and survive. But the Indian people will not tolerate a dictatorship for long."

Tipped off to secret meetings of small resistance groups, police raided private homes. Torture was used to extract confessions of an alleged plot against Mrs. Gandhi. Some victims were hung upside down, stripped naked and beaten with steel rods and gun butts.

Legislation rammed through the Indian Parliament by Mrs. Gandhi now made retroactively legal the illegal campaign activities of which she had been accused. The Supreme Court then cleared her of the charges. The Court also obliged by upholding her right to jail her opponents without the right to a hearing. "Liberty . . . is not an absolute freedom," explained Chief Justice A. N. Ray.

As though to illustrate his ruling, Mrs. Gandhi, who believes in compulsory sterilization to reduce India's ruinous birthrate, used her emergency powers to permit men in Maharashtra to be seized on the streets, thrown into garbage trucks and forced to submit to sterilization operations on the spot!

When the government of the southern state of Tamil Nadu opposed her dictatorship, Mrs. Gandhi dismissed the government and imposed direct rule from New Delhi. Hundreds of the state's elected representatives were arrested and jailed.

The new police state achieved some economic successes in improving India's shaky economy. By forbidding strikes and bonuses, a soaring inflation was halted. Food prices were forced down by 20%, helped by a good harvest. Smuggling and currency speculation were curbed. Some slums in New Delhi were cleared. These and other reforms increased Mrs. Gandhi's popularity among India's impoverished peasants, who were more concerned with better economic conditions than with political freedom.

One Indian official said seriously, "Indira had to destroy democracy in India in order to save it."

The censorship imposed by India, as by police states around the world, became so grave a problem that a London editor, Michael Scammell, began publishing a quarterly *Index on Censorship* devoted to the defense of freedom of expression. It still provides an outlet for suppressed manuscripts smuggled out of police states from Moscow to East Berlin to Santiago. Scammell saw the temporary defection of India, the second largest nation in the world, from the ranks of the democracies as a severely damaging blow to world freedom.

"Before these events, the Indian press was totally free," he explained. "India was a shining exception to the rule of a controlled press in Asia. . . ." Luckily, new elections in 1977 deposed Mrs. Gandhi and restored democracy to India.

Still, with more and more of the world's governments becoming repressive police states, we cannot avoid facing the obvious and ominous question, incredible as the idea may now seem:

Could it happen here, too?

VII

Could It Happen Here?

We have so far managed to remain the democracy we were born on July 4, 1776, and have even improved it by broadening it to improve the rights of women, the poor, blacks and other minorities. But there have been times in our history when American administrations resorted to police-state tactics. We might do well to examine those times. "Those who cannot remember the past," warned philosopher George Santayana, "are condemned to repeat it."

When John Adams became the second President of the United States, in 1797, the country became polarized between two political parties. Federalists, the majority party, were opposed by the minority Democrat Republicans, led by Vice-President Thomas Jefferson.

By 1798 there were 25,000 refugees of the French Revolution in the United States. They were joined that year by Catholic refugees from an unsuccessful rebellion in Ireland. Almost all the immigrants vigorously supported Jefferson against the Adams administration. Adams took a dim view of these "treasonous aliens." He also feared their votes, which he knew might help elect Jefferson and the Democrat Republicans.

So Adams's Federalist Congress passed the Alien and Sedition Acts of 1798. The Acts made immigrants wait 14 years instead of 5 to become voting citizens. They also gave Adams power to deport by executive decree foreigners suspected of violating the Acts, without the need of specifying charges or holding a trial or hearing. This threat of expulsion was enough to silence his French and Irish critics, who also feared to join or support the Democrat Republicans.

Worse, the Acts made it an offense punishable by fine or imprisonment to speak or write against the President or Congress "with the intent to defame," or to bring them "into contempt or disrepute." This provision was aimed directly at Jefferson and his followers. Adams had made political opposition the equivalent of treason.

Alarmed Democrat Republicans branded this repressive legislation a clear violation of the Bill of Rights. Congressman Matthew Lyon of Vermont called Adams a democracy-hating aristocrat. He was promptly arrested, fined a thousand dollars and sent to jail for 4 months. For denouncing this political persecution, Vermont's Anthony Haswell was fined $200 and imprisoned for 2 months. David Brown, a Massachusetts politician who organized a protest demonstration, was sentenced to prison for 4 years. Democrat Republican editors were silenced by heavy fines or jail sentences. Frightened Frenchmen fled back to France.

The Federalists introduced another bill that would have made it an act of treason to speak against the Sedition Law. Federalist judges raged at lawyers who dared defend its victims in court, branding them "traitors to their country."

Fortunately for Americans, Adams did not attempt to extend his powers by suppressing elections and seeking to cling to office as a dictator. And, angered by the Federalists' threat to democracy, Americans voted Adams out of office and Jefferson in. Those oppressive Alien and Sedition Acts that did not automatically expire were instantly repealed, and their victims were released from prison.

Another serious threat to our democracy occurred when the Bill of Rights was set aside by an American President during the Civil War. Abraham Lincoln wielded greater power than any other President until Franklin D. Roosevelt. He was, in fact, a wartime dictator. Without prior approval of Congress, he called for a draft into the Union Army, and declared a blockade of the South, in violation of Article I, Section 8, of the Constitution.

The North was far from united on the decision to go to war with the South. Many prominent Northerners and residents of border states either sympathized with the South or wanted their states to stay neutral. When resistance welled up in Maryland, Lincoln issued a Presidential proclamation suspending the right of habeas corpus, which prevents arbitrary imprisonment and requires the liberation of anyone being held in jail illegally.

Lincoln's order permitted any Northern general "to arrest and detain without resort to the ordinary procedures of law such individuals as he might deem dangerous to the public safety." It violated Section 9 of Article I of the Constitution, which states, "The privilege of the writ of habeas corpus shall not be suspended, unless when in cases of rebellion or invasion the public safety may require it."

But Lincoln insisted that his proclamation was constitutional because of the public safety clause. The Union, he argued, was in danger of collapsing because of the refusal of almost a third of the states to obey the laws of the nation.

"These rebels are violating the Constitution to destroy the Union," he declared. "I will violate the Constitution, if necessary, to save the Union." He termed the right of habeas corpus a law "made in such extreme tenderness of the citizen's liberty, that, practically, it relieves more of the guilty than the innocent." And he asked, "Are all the laws but one to go unexecuted, and the government itself go to pieces, lest that one be violated?"

But that one law protected Americans against police-state persecution. When it was suspended, a mayor of Baltimore, suspected of Southern sympathies, was arrested and confined without trial in a fortress for over a year. A Maryland judge who instructed a grand jury to investigate illegal acts by government officials was dragged off his court bench, beaten bloody, and jailed for 6 months.

These were not isolated instances. "Public safety" became a catch-all clause any general could use against political figures he disliked, civilians whose opinions or actions he disapproved of, or his personal enemies. (In our own century, such use has often been made of the notion of "national security.")

Many Northerners were also infuriated by Lincoln's draft proclamation. Any civilian resisting the draft, discouraging enlistment, or "guilty of any disloyal practice affording aid and comfort to rebels" could be tried by the military or held in jail arbitrarily. Outrageous, said Lincoln's critics. Were Americans free or not?

The Supreme Court heard the appeal of one civilian who had been arrested and court-martialed in a district where civil courts were open. The Court decided (ex parte *Milligan*) that the President's assumed war powers had violated his constitutional rights. But by then the war was over. It was too late to help any of over 13,000 Americans who had been imprisoned by what amounted to a military dictatorship.

Like Adams, however, Lincoln was no would-be dictator. As soon as the Civil War was over, the constitutional rights of the people were restored.

2

The problem of wartime dictatorship is nothing new for democracies. The first dictator appeared in the Roman Republic of 501 B.C. He was a deputy appointed by the two consuls who governed Rome when they had to be absent leading armies to war. The dictator ruled without regard to Roman law. Accepting such rule as a wartime necessity, the Romans nevertheless refused to allow any dictator to hold office for more than six months.

When President Woodrow Wilson took America into World War I in April 1917, he silenced all opposition by having Congress pass first the Espionage Act, then the Sedition Act. Anyone uttering "disloyal or abusive" language about the government, the Constitution, the flag or the uniform could be punished by $20,000 fines and jail terms up to 20 years. The laws were an ominous echo of the oppressive Alien and Sedition Acts engineered by John Adams. The Postmaster General was also authorized to ban from the mails any newspapers or periodicals he judged to be "unpatriotic."

Among 1,500 Americans arrested for "disloyalty" were members of the Socialist and other Marxist political parties, pacifists, anarchists, "hyphenated Americans" (German- and Irish-Americans who had no love for America's British allies), and cynics who labeled the war a struggle for markets between English and German capitalists.

The rights of freedom of speech guaranteed in the First Amendment went out the window. Socialist leader Eugene Debs was sentenced to jail for 10 years, and deprived of his citizenship, for making speeches opposing the war as an imperialist conflict for markets and profits. He ran for President against Wilson from his jail cell.

"The court of final resort is the people," Debs said hopefully, "and that court will be heard in due time." He received almost a million votes. Unlike Lincoln, who pardoned jailed opponents of the war as soon as it was over, Wilson refused to forgive Debs, denying him a postwar pardon.

The Wilson administration's enforcement of the Espionage and Sedition Acts was arbitrary and brutal. One St. Louis woman went to jail for 10 years for writing in a letter to a newspaper, "I am for the people and the Government is for the profiteers." Other sentences included 15 years for talking against the draft; 10 years for opposing the government's Liberty Loan fund-raising drives; 20 years for calling the government a liar and predicting a German victory.

Wilson's Attorney General, A. Mitchell Palmer, took the view that *all* "radically inclined individuals," not merely Communists, were dangerous to the security of the United States. He sent 100 Federal agents without legal search warrants to raid labor-union offices in 50 cities, seizing their files, arresting labor leaders and indicting them for alleged violations of the Espionage Act.

Following the war, Palmer ordered his aide, J. Edgar Hoover, who had compiled a list of 60,000 "suspected radicals," to organize new raids in 33 cities. Over 10,000 political and labor militants were seized in mass arrests, along with their files.

Ostensibly, Palmer sought to "prevent" a radical revolution in the United States similar to the Communist Revolution that had turned Russia into the Soviet Union a year earlier. Labor, however, saw the raids as an attempt to intimidate union leaders and keep them from calling postwar strikes protesting low wages, high prices and unemployment.

The raiders hauled aliens and citizens alike from their beds, dragged them out of meetings and seized them on the streets. In Detroit 800 people were held for days in a windowless corridor with only one toilet and no sink or bathtub. After being held for weeks incommunicado, often brutally beaten, many were sentenced to up to 14 years in prison on flimsy or trumped-up charges. Union halls were shut down, labor newspapers suppressed. Some 249 "undesirable" aliens were forcibly deported to the Soviet Union.

Felix Frankfurter, who had been chairman of the War Labor Policies Board, joined a dozen prominent lawyers in condemning the Palmer raids as the acts of a police state. "Under the guise of a campaign for the suppression of radical activities," they charged, "the office of the Attorney General . . . has committed illegal acts. Wholesale arrests of both aliens and citizens have been made without warrant or any due process of law; men and women have been jailed and held incommunicado without access of friends and counsel; homes have been entered without search warrant and property seized and removed; workingmen and workingwomen suspected of radical views have been shamefully abused and maltreated . . . all at the expense of the government and outside the scope of the Attorney General's duties."

Furious, Palmer attacked the lawyers as "Communists." He added the name of Frankfurter to J. Edgar Hoover's list of suspected subversives, which grew until it included 450,000 names. (Years later Felix Frankfurter became one of America's most celebrated Supreme Court justices.)

Hysterical government dread of American radicalism faded with the end of the Wilson administration. It did not die out completely, but at least police-state tactics in the name of "preventing a Communist takeover" were discredited. The Constitution was once more permitted to protect the liberties of those who opposed the government.

3

A decade later a little-known episode in our history involved a plot to take over the government by a coup d'etat and transform it into a police state. The conspirators were a group of some of the most powerful men in America.

The plot had its origins in the stock-market crash of 1929. The subsequent Depression created an army of 15 million unemployed. Unable to meet mortgage or rent payments, families were evicted from homes and apartments. Farm prices fell so low that it was costing farmers more to transport their produce than they would get paid for it. So they let fruit rot in the orchards, dumped milk on the highway and destroyed livestock, while hungry men searched garbage cans outside restaurants for rotten fruit and meat scraps. Food riots broke out in many cities.

Elections in 1932 resulted in a crushing defeat for the Republican administration that had permitted the country to fall into such economic chaos. Voters elected Democratic President Franklin D. Roosevelt, who promised to take immediate steps to end the country's plight, and did.

He initiated a series of programs to try to correct everything that had gone wrong. Under his New Deal, the government spent huge sums to feed the hungry, create jobs, and save the homes, farms and small businesses from being lost.

But bankers and industrialists grew convinced that Roosevelt was following a program of "creeping Socialism" that would bankrupt them and the country.

One powerful group of Right-wing extremists, representing America's corporate giants, met secretly to consult on what could be done to stop "that man in the White House." They decided on a military putsch to seize the White House and install a Right-wing dictator of their own choice.

Having no experience in so dangerous an enterprise, they sent agent Gerald C. MacGuire to Europe to study several police states as models. When he returned, he presented a plan to seize power with a private American army of veterans. At least half the membership of all U.S. veterans' organizations could be quickly enlisted, MacGuire was certain, if the right general led the paramilitary army.

The one man he was confident could do it was Smedley Darlington Butler, an enormously popular war hero. MacGuire was sure he could convince General Butler that a coup d'etat would be an act of the highest patriotism, saving the country from Communism.

The wealthy plotters agreed to put up as much as $300 million, if necessary, to raise a veterans' army of over half a million men and stage a march on Washington.

Fortunately for Americans, General Butler was a genuine patriot resolutely devoted to the principles of democracy. He pretended to consider the proposal of the wealthy conspirators until he had learned sufficient details of the plot and the identities of the conspirators. He then exposed the conspiracy in sworn testimony before the McCormack-Dickstein Committee of the House of Representatives —HUAC, the original House Un-American Activities Committee. Alarmed at revelations of their intended treason, the conspirators quickly abandoned their plans, and the affair was hushed up.

So the plot to turn America Fascist fizzled, but John W. McCormack, later Speaker of the House, emphasized that it might have succeeded if General Butler had relished the role of American dictator.

4

Soon after World War II, during the period known as the Cold War, American fears were aroused over the possible aggressive intentions of the Soviet Union. This led to another witch-hunt reminiscent of the Palmer Raid hysteria that followed World War I. The Republican party, seeking popular political issues to win the White House from the Democrats, accused them of "twenty years of treason." The administration of President Harry S. Truman was charged with being "riddled with Communists."

In March 1947 Truman bowed to political pressure by issuing a Loyalty Order subjecting 2 million Federal employees to a purge of suspected Communists or "fellow travelers"—nonmembers believed sympathetic to the party. Over 3,000 were removed from their jobs for holding views considered too radical. Another 8,000 were forced out of their jobs under a cloud of suspicion. The loyalty probes extended everywhere—into the armed forces, universities with government research grants, industrial plants with defense contracts.

Congressional committees staged headline-winning investigations of government officials, Hollywood stars, writers, teachers, labor leaders and others. Attempts were made to smear them as subversive, on flimsy circumstantial evidence such as their having attended parties at which Communists were present. Their Constitutional rights disregarded, they were pilloried in a way that would assure their being fired or boycotted in their professions as "un-American."

146

The House Un-American Activities Committee was the chief instrument for these police-state tactics. HUAC refused to allow those accused as Communists to cross-examine their accusers, some of whom were paid informers with prison records. Many of the accused were merely liberals whose reputations were unjustly tarnished. Famous novelist Thomas Mann, a refugee from Nazi Germany, warned against such political inquisitions. "That is how it started in Germany," he reminded Americans. "What followed was Fascism."

"The most un-American activity in the United States today," noted a Detroit *Free Press* editorial, "is the conduct of the congressional committee on un-American activities."

A climate of repression spread across the nation. The National Education Association found that by July 1949 some 22 states had adopted loyalty laws requiring the firing of any teachers who uttered "treasonable" or "subversive" remarks. One teacher asked sarcastically, "Is it all right to quote from the Declaration of Independence?"

HUAC's chief investigator turned over a "suspect" list of 3,000 teachers, 1,000 clergymen and half a million other Americans to Republican Senator Joseph McCarthy of Wisconsin. McCarthy, an unscrupulous, politically ambitious demagogue, used it in a Senate witch-hunt that outdid even HUAC in finding "Red traitors" everywhere, especially in government.

His favorite gambit was waving a piece of paper and declaring, "I have here a list of 205 names made known to the Secretary of State as members of the Communist party, who are nevertheless now shaping policy in the State Department." Sometimes he declared the number of names on his never-shown list to be 57; at other times it became 81.

Leading Americans, including clergymen, who advocated peace, civil rights or social reform were smeared as "treasonous agents of Moscow." McCarthy called upon all government employees to inform on one another, and on department heads, if they suspected anyone of Communist beliefs or tendencies.

"There won't be enough cells in Federal prisons when I get through!" he boasted. His threat was backed by the Senate's McCarran Act of 1950, which required registration of Communist and

"Communist-front" organizations with the Department of Justice. It also provided for the internment of subversives during a "national emergency" in six concentration camps with a capacity of 100,000 persons.

President Truman vetoed the bill. "The application of the registration requirements to so-called Communist-front organizations," he declared, "can be the greatest danger to freedom of speech, press and assembly since the Alien and Sedition laws of 1798." Congress passed the bill over his veto. "Jefferson," noted *Christian Century*, "would have gone to jail."

The election of a Republican President, Dwight D. Eisenhower, in 1952 did not deter McCarthy from continuing his inquisitional reign of terror against free thought. The hysteria he whipped up lit flames of intolerance across the land. "A spirit of fear and dread blanketed the nation," said historian Gustavus Myers, "and everywhere 'little McCarthys' sprang up to accuse, threaten and terrorize their fellow countrymen."

McCarthy finally overreached himself by starting an investigation of "Communism in the Army." Sensational hearings in the spring of 1954 were televised to 20 million fascinated Americans who, for the first time, saw McCarthy in action. They were shocked by the way he sneered at and bullied witnesses, many clearly innocent of the outrageous charges he flung at them. The tide of public opinion turned rapidly.

Bewildered, McCarthy found himself suddenly discredited and scorned. In December, by a vote of 67 to 22, the Senate passed a resolution of censure against him. President Eisenhower publicly congratulated the Senate on its good judgment. McCarthy's reign of terror was over. It was once more safe for Americans to believe in and trust the Bill of Rights.

5

Meanwhile J. Edgar Hoover, by now head of the Federal Bureau of Investigation (FBI) which was authorized to investigate violations of Federal laws, had developed that division of the Department of Justice into a powerful national spy force. Beginning with the World

War II years, for five Presidential administrations the FBI compiled secret dossiers, conducted surveillance and installed wiretaps, largely against Left-wing spokesmen and political figures opposing the administration in power.

Hoover's collected files of information included dossiers on Congressmen which contained embarrassing secrets obtained by bugging their phones. He let their existence be known, as a form of blackmail, with the result that few Congressmen dared criticize his methods or cut funds from his huge budget. Instead they joined a sycophantic chorus of praise for Hoover as a great folk hero, which most of the media slavishly repeated. Hoover and the FBI became American legends, perpetuated by radio and TV programs that celebrated their role as crime fighters and were silent about FBI violations of the Bill of Rights.

At a Senate hearing in 1954 it was revealed that in the two preceding years alone, 24,000 Americans had had their mail tampered with illegally.

Later, between 1960 and 1966, the FBI broke into the offices of the Socialist Workers party (SWP), a small, peaceful, legal radical group, 92 different times, photographing some 10,000 documents in the party's files. The party sued the government. The Justice Department at first denied charges that FBI agents had burglarized SWP offices. But *The New York Times* revealed that FBI officials, while admitting that the SWP was nonviolent, "have defended their attempts to disrupt the party on the ground that there was no assurance that its members might not one day embrace violence." *Might!*

Another government agency busy violating the law in police-state fashion was the Central Intelligence Agency. The CIA is set up by law to gather only foreign intelligence for the guidance of American foreign policy. Instead, it has also operated as a domestic espionage agency, carrying out clandestine activities between 1940 and 1973 that the government feigned to know nothing about.

During this period the CIA joined the FBI in illegally opening and photographing letters at the post office (215,820 letters in New York City alone). Their copies were filed, indexed and secretly made available to other intelligence organizations, the Attorney General and the President. Among their chief targets were militant black leaders and opponents of the war in Vietnam. One CIA snooping program opened the mail of senators, congressmen, journalists, businessmen and even a Presidential candidate.

The CIA also conducted a series of secret programs labeled CHAOS, MERRIMAC and RESISTANCE to spy domestically, beginning in 1967, on American dissidents. CHAOS amassed hundreds of thousands of computer records on antiwar protesters. Project MERRIMAC spied on militant black and peace groups to build dossiers on their leaders, money sources, policies and activities. Project RESISTANCE spied on radical groups, particularly on campuses, to build files on anti-CIA activists.

6

The war effort which their energies were expended in protecting was America's intervention in the civil war in Vietnam. During the 1960's President Lyndon B. Johnson sent more than half a million Americans to fight on behalf of the Right-wing government of South Vietnam, against the Communist government of North Vietnam.

Widespread opposition to the war was expressed by protest marches, draft resistance riots and firebombings. But police and army troops often failed to distinguish between the right of legitimate, peaceful protest and illegal, violent protest. Often when a few hotheaded demonstrators threw missiles—and sometimes even when they didn't—police and troops would break up the demonstrations brutally with swinging clubs, tear gas and weapons fire. Many angry American youths grew disillusioned with the government's abuse of their rights of free speech and assembly.

Blacks were especially alienated, because the President, while drafting large numbers of blacks for service in Vietnam, cut back promised appropriations to improve life in the ghettos, spending more billions instead on the war. Protesting, they were harshly manhandled by police. Young armed black militants led urban uprisings. Many American cities were plunged into turmoil by civil disorder, looting, gun battles and fires.

The President grew weary of the crisis that had boiled up in the backlash of the Vietnam War. Realizing that he could not be reelected, he announced that he would not run in the 1968 elections. Dissent, in effect, drove him from office, indicating that the American democratic process *was* still working despite attempts by the administration to suppress opposition.

Richard M. Nixon, the Republican candidate in the 1968 elections, assured voters that he would end American involvement in the Vietnam War within 6 months. He also appealed to middle-class voters alienated by riots and demonstrations, promising to restore law and order and bind up America's wounds. Nixon won the election.

Once in office, however, he proved as unwilling to end the disastrous intervention in Vietnam as President Johnson had been. "I do not intend to become the first President to preside over an American defeat," he declared. Repudiation of his campaign promise inflamed antiwar activists, who resumed their protest demonstrations on a magnified scale.

Nixon attempted to discredit the antiwar movement by discovering links between it and overseas Communism. The FBI, CIA and other government intelligence agencies were ordered to investigate and keep files on Americans—including even Congressmen—involved in antiwar activities.

Students in the forefront of the antiwar movement were prime targets. Over half the nation's schools and universities permitted Federal agents to see student records. In one instance a 16-year-old girl, Lori Paton, was investigated by the FBI for subversion because she wrote a letter to a Socialist party for information she needed as part of a school project. When her indignant parents sued the government for this infringement of her rights, the FBI backed off hastily, claiming an error.

In addition to spying on antiadministration groups, FBI agents infiltrated some to provoke violence. To discredit them with the public, the agents provided dissenters with grenades, offered training in explosives and firearms, encouraged draft-board break-ins to destroy records and spurred attacks on police. Later hearings revealed that they had even engineered street warfare between militant black organizations, using forgery, lies and other frauds to get them to destroy each other violently.

The Justice Department arrested and indicted many protest leaders on charges of "conspiracy," a tactic tying up dissidents in legal proceedings. (But since most of the evidence had been obtained illegally, the majority of the cases were ultimately dismissed.)

Although the CIA joined the FBI in spying on dissenting Americans, it reported honestly that it could find no evidence of any Communist conspiracy masterminded abroad, as President Nixon insisted, but that the antiwar movement stemmed only from legal, political opposition by American youth. The White House was extremely dissatisfied with these reports.

Accordingly, the President sought to take direct control of all Federal investigative agencies, attempting to put them under a single police force operating from the White House. The plan failed, however, when FBI Director J. Edgar Hoover refused to give up his independent power. But Nixon persisted in various schemes to set up his own secret political police force.

The White House also mobilized thirty groups of supporters around the country to inhibit freedom of expression by the news media, because the President considered the media prejudiced against him. He had the Justice Department file antitrust suits against the three major TV networks, seeking to pressure them into censoring unfavorable news and comment about Nixon, and to force newsmen to present him in a flattering light. White House aides also threatened tax troubles for executives who did not yield to their demands. "The harder I pressed them," Presidential aide Charles Colson reported, "the more accommodating, cordial and almost apologetic they became. . . . They are damned nervous and scared, and we should continue to take a very tough line."

CBS correspondent Dan Rather reported that the White House was spending $400 million a year of taxpayers' money to glorify Nixon. He and other outspoken newsmen were placed under FBI surveillance as "enemies" of the President. But they refused to be intimidated.

When Nixon widened the war in Vietnam by invading Cambodia in 1970, the nation's universities erupted in protest demonstrations. Four students were killed at Kent State University in Ohio by National Guardsmen. Horrified students and faculty were forbidden to gather on the campus to mourn them publicly.

"What really struck me," one professor said afterward, "was that my rights were taken away, just like that. I saw how tenuous our rights really are, even in this so-called democratic country. If you can't have your freedom of assembly, your freedom of speech is curtailed."

But Nixon's attempts at repressing dissent continued to backfire. Students at over 440 universities called strikes to protest the killing of the Kent State students. The National Student Association demanded the impeachment of the President.

Half a million angry Americans staged a protest march on Washington against his expansion of the war into Cambodia. Nixon's Attorney General, John Mitchell, ordered police to make mass arrests in the name of "national security." Over 13,000 citizens were arrested and detained overnight in outdoor stockades. (A Federal court later ruled this action illegal and ordered the government to pay damages to those citizens improperly detained.)

Acting on President Nixon's orders, J. Edgar Hoover organized a new "security index" of 10,000 political dissenters who became the targets of aggressive FBI investigations. Republican Senator Lowell Weicker of Connecticut bitterly protested that FBI agents, "unaware that they are servants of the people, have intimidated, threatened and harassed individuals and groups. Some have used police-state techniques."

One peace group calling itself the Citizens' Committee to Investigate the FBI upset Hoover and the President by breaking into an FBI office in Media, Pennsylvania. They pilfered documents proving that fully 40% of the FBI's activities involved political harassment rather than being devoted entirely to law enforcement, which was its legal authority.

Antiwar congressmen were outraged when they discovered that they were also being followed around by Army military intelligence agents who reported on the people they met with and what they said in speeches.

By this time the President was using ten Federal agencies and departments, employing about 150,000 people, to feed the White House political intelligence on Americans who opposed his policies.

The dossiers collected on them multiplied rapidly in computers and data banks, cross-referenced for easy use.

Senator Frank Church, whose committee later investigated the CIA's "police-state" tactics, found that the agency, in addition to spying on Americans at home, had over a period of six administrations (1) overthrown the government of Guatemala; (2) sought to overthrow the government of Indonesia; (3) restored the Shah to the throne of Iran; (4) sought to overthrow and assassinate Castro; (5) sought to poison Congo leader Patrice Lumumba; (6) conducted a secret war in Laos; (7) aided in assassinating Rafael Trujillo of the Dominican Republic; (8) aided in the ouster and murder of South Vietnam's Premier Ngo Dinh Diem; (9) interfered in the Chilean election, then helped overthrow the government, leading to the murder of Allende. All of these warlike acts had been perpetrated without the knowledge or consent of Congress, in violation of the Constitution.

When some CIA secrets were exposed, CIA Director Richard Helms made a speech to the National Press Club. "You've just got to trust us," he implored the reporters. "We are honorable men." Senator Sam Ervin accused the administration of a "Gestapo mentality."

"The dossiers generated by a police-state apparatus may be few, inaccurate and incomplete," noted Senator Weicker, "but the process of gathering them can crush dissent."

"The truth is," said Supreme Court Justice William O. Douglas, "that wiretapping today is a plague on the nation."

7

When the press began publishing news stories revealing the embarrassing secrets of the Nixon administration, the President feared his chances for reelection might be crippled. He ordered security tightened, with increased wiretapping of government officials and newsmen to discover the sources of the news leaks and stop them.

Public opinion polls indicated that Nixon was likely to lose the 1972 elections to the Democrats. Alarmed, the President and his men resorted to political sabotage to wreck the Democratic party's campaign. A secret investigative unit known as the Plumbers was set up in the White House. It was instructed to burglarize offices, steal papers, bug phones and do anything else necessary to get compromising information on the President's opponents.

The White House also ordered the Bureau of Internal Revenue to set up a "Special Service" staff to harass, by tax audits, still another "enemies list" maintained by the President's aides. A later Congressional investigation denounced this punitive use of the tax machinery as an "improper and indeed dangerous use of Government power against the citizenry of this nation."

The plan of the President and his men to steal the election ran into trouble. On June 19, 1972, the Plumbers, working out of Nixon's campaign-committee headquarters, were caught red-handed burglarizing and bugging Democratic party headquarters in Washington's Watergate office building. They were instantly disowned by both the Committee to Reelect the President (CRP) and the White House.

Two *Washington Post* reporters, Carl Bernstein and Bob Woodward, nevertheless persisted in probing the mystery surrounding the arrest of the Plumbers. The President and his men were aware that if the Plumbers talked, the truth about other break-ins ordered by the White House could also leak out. These revelations would surely turn voters against the President on Election Day. Nixon and his aides not only bribed the Plumbers to stay silent, but even destroyed evidence linking them to the White House. They also blocked an FBI investigation of the case.

Because they managed to keep the country from realizing the truth about their secret political crimes, Richard Nixon was reelected in 1972. He now had four more years to complete the concentration of government power into his own hands.

But reporters Bernstein and Woodward would not be shaken off the story, despite White House pressure on the management of *The Washington Post.* In the best tradition of the American free press, they exposed one secret after another of the Watergate scandal. They revealed that the Plumbers had acted under orders of the former Attorney General, John Mitchell, who had resigned to head Nixon's reelection committee, CRP. They found evidence that both this committee and the White House had paid the Plumbers hush money out of campaign funds.

These and other revelations by the *Post* shocked the nation.

"A large number of Americans, both in the general populace and at the highest levels of government, are behaving as if we already had a police state in America," worried Senator Weicker in May 1973. "What we are witnessing is the development of a style of repression that is new to us, the establishment in this country of conditions—technological, psychological and legal—making government by police state possible through an apparatus of total surveillance that seldom would need the reinforcement of a political trial."

Former Democratic Senator Wayne Morse of Oregon also warned his countrymen, "What you are faced with is the steady erosion of the Constitutional safeguards of the American people. The result is that we are fast approaching a police state; we are getting ominously close to where the German people stood just before Hitler's Third Reich."

At first, many Americans refused to believe the truth about President Nixon and his aides, who indignantly denied any involvement. In private, however, they held frantic conferences seeking to cover up everything they had done to suppress the truth about the Watergate affair. The acting director of the FBI was ordered to destroy crucial evidence.

These attempts at cover-up were thwarted when the Senate decided to hold public hearings. The President was dealt a second setback after one arrested Plumber, James McCord, offered to tell everything he knew in return for a more lenient sentence. Alarmed, Nixon ordered all his aides and bureau chiefs to refuse to testify either in Congress or in court on grounds of "national security." Such testimony, he argued, would reveal secret information which would be harmful to our interests if Communist nations learned about it.

But then the President's White House counsel, John Dean, decided to save his own skin by testifying truthfully before the Senate Watergate Committee headed by Sam Ervin. The Nixon Administration's secrets began tumbling out into the news media. The President realized that the cat was now hopelessly out of the bag. He desperately sought to escape the disgrace of being impeached by the House and tried by the Senate to remove him from office if found guilty of criminal acts. With his aides he now conspired to conceal all their attempts to obstruct justice by stopping the investigations. But the Senate compelled Nixon to appoint a special prosecutor with the power to subpoena all evidence.

Meanwhile, the Senate hearings revealed that the President had made secret tape recordings of all his White House conversations. Nixon refused to surrender any of these tapes either to the Special Prosecutor or the Senate Watergate Committee. But they contained vital evidence that could prove the guilt or innocence of everyone in the White House, including the President.

Nixon insisted that the tapes must remain secret because of "national security" and the President's traditional right of "confidentiality." These claims were rejected by the courts, and he finally agreed to surrender some tapes. On one, 18 minutes of a crucial conversation were found to have been erased by—the White House explained lamely—"a terrible mistake." The Special Prosecutor then demanded more of the tapes. Angered, the President fired him.

This was the last straw for Congress. Its House Judiciary Committee (HJC) began hearings to decide whether the President should be impeached. The whole country watched their bipartisan debates on TV. Nixon swore to Republican members of the HJC that he was personally innocent of all Watergate-related crimes. They sought to save him, at first, by insisting that there was no hard evidence to prove he had personally participated in the conspiracies.

But a newly appointed Special Prosecutor compelled the President to turn over the White House tapes that provided clear proof of his personal guilt by revealing that despite his repeated denials, he had personally participated in the conspiracy to cover up the Watergate crimes.

Americans now learned that Nixon had been lying to them about burglaries his administration had authorized. That he and his closest aides had accepted bribes in the form of campaign contributions. That he had cheated on his income taxes and spent public funds on his private estates. That he had hired thugs to commit criminal acts.

That he had obstructed the processes of justice by destroying evidence and authorizing blackmail payments, and by derailing the FBI investigations of the Watergate break-in. That Mr. Nixon and his men had invaded citizens' privacy by wiretapping and bugging, spying on members of Congress as well. That they had violated citizens' rights by keeping secret files on them. That they had used agents to spy on, disrupt and incite domestic political groups to violence. That they had intercepted, opened and read private mail. That they had used poison-pen letters and other unsavory tactics against critics. That they had urged everyone who could implicate the President to commit perjury instead. That they had illegally misused the power of government agencies—the FBI, CIA and Internal Revenue Service.

It was obvious that there had to be a high-level investigation of those in high places responsible, not just a scapegoat trial of the "small-fry" Plumbers who had been caught. Shocked, even his supporters on the HJC now voted to recommend his impeachment. Not even a handful of Republicans in the Senate, which would hold the impeachment trial of the President, was prepared to defend him.

It was now inevitable that he would be found guilty of what the Constitution calls "high crimes and misdemeanors," and removed from the White House in disgrace. Cornered, he resigned rather than face the Senate trial. Becoming the first American President in history to be driven out of office, he was also spared criminal indictment by a pardon granted to him by his hand-picked successor, the new President, Gerald Ford. Only the President's chief aides were tried and convicted.

Senator Weicker called the fallen President and his aides "the men who almost stole America."

* * * * *

The Watergate affair made the American people aware of the danger that an unscrupulous use of police-state suppression and espionage tactics by a President could threaten our whole democratic system. Subsequent investigations disclosed that previous Presidents had also used such tactics, a revelation Nixon's defenders were quick to seize upon to argue that his principal error was not one of unique criminality but of getting caught.

But this claim was hardly impressive in excusing the conduct of the chief officer of the United States, especially since his abuse of the laws was far more extensive and persistent than the occasional misconduct of some other Presidents.

Nixon had attempted to establish what historian Arthur Schlesinger has termed "the imperial Presidency," by making the President's executive powers supreme over the other two branches of government. His defenders argued that this attempt was not unique. Franklin D. Roosevelt had also sought to do the same, to the extent of trying (and failing) to reorganize the Supreme Court so that it could not nullify his legislation as unconstitutional.

With that exception, however, no other President had ever tried, as Nixon did, to bypass the powers of Congress and the courts. It was a tribute to the strength of the democratic system that he had failed in his desperate, ominous effort. Almost all his attempts to persecute his political opponents and cover up his violations of law were nullified by court and Congressional actions that defeated them.

"Among the principal lessons of Watergate and Vietnam," observed the American Civil Liberties Union, "are that secrecy in government is cancerous to our democracy, and dissent is healthy."

It was now apparent that no future President could be allowed to hold himself beyond or above the law, if we were to remain a government under law and not one in which the people's rights could be ignored or taken away by one man's edicts.

8

This brief review of times when our democracy came under attack from within indicates that the United States is not immune to the pressures that in other parts of the world have resulted in the loss of political freedom. We can take pride that our system has been strong enough to withstand such pressures for over two centuries. But because such pressures will increase in proportion to the grave problems that lie ahead of us as a people, we cannot relax on the assumption that we could never become a police state. We could—given a crisis of grave proportions and a frightened population.

The separation of powers is the cornerstone of American democracy. Those who wrote our Constitution carefully divided these powers among the executive, legislative and judicial branches of government.

"Neither the mushrooming surveillance technology nor the FBI's aggressive intelligence gathering makes America a police state," former Senator Charles Goodell pointed out. "The outcome depends on what the highest officials of the Executive Branch of our government choose to do with the potential for political control inherent in the apparatus. . . . The people of this country should realize it is in the plurality of their institutions that the greatest safeguards exist."

We must, in other words, carefully watch any President who seeks to set his own powers above those of Congress and the courts. We must carefully watch all investigative agencies like the FBI and CIA, to make sure they operate within the boundaries of the law with full respect for the rights of every citizen. We must prevent any infringement of those rights by President or police, as well as any attempt to write new laws that would abolish those rights.

"A constitutional government," Mortimer J. Adler and William Gorman wrote in their book *The American Testament*, ". . . must see to it that law enforcement is itself lawful . . . its conduct subject to steady, critical, and politically accountable examination by the people."

We must never allow any administration, for whatever reason, to ban the right of dissent. Freedom is the right to disagree with our government openly, without fear of being silenced, penalized, clubbed, arrested or tortured. Without that right we are not citizens of a free state, but subjects of a police state.

"The price of lawful public dissent," said the Supreme Court in 1972, "must not be a dread of subjection to an unchecked surveillance power. Nor must the fear of unauthorized official eavesdropping deter vigorous citizen dissent and discussion of Government action in private conversation. For private dissent, no less than open public discourse, is essential to our free society."

We need to be thoroughly educated in the principles on which our

160

nation is founded. One Pasadena high school announced, "In the tenth grade, study is concentrated on the growth of democracy. . . . Such a study should be brief and to the point, in order to allow time for driver education."

What would Thomas Jefferson have thought of *that*?

No matter how discouraged we may get about the Kennedy and Johnson administrations that gave us Vietnam, then the Nixon administration that gave us more Vietnam plus Watergate, we cannot allow ourselves to despair of politics. It was just such despair that caused the German people to turn to Adolf Hitler and dictatorship. While there is freedom, there is hope that we will all learn to make wiser choices of the candidates we select to run our government.

Even if we make mistakes in the men we put in the White House, those mistakes need not be fatal, provided our Presidents are always counterbalanced by the two other powerful branches of government —Congress and the Supreme Court. *And as long as we protect the right no police state permits—to elect a new administration every four years.*

Youth often feels frustrated and powerless to "turn the Establishment around." But is such pessimism really justified? It was the youth of America, after all, who stirred the dissent that compelled the government of the United States to end its tragic involvement in Vietnam, and to stop the violations of democracy it brought.

The turmoil of the 1960's proved that student power could be stronger than the police-state tactics of a war-minded government. As Mario Savio, a student leader of that time, put it: "There's a time when the operation of the machine becomes so odious, makes you so sick at heart that you can't take part. And you've got to put your bodies upon the gears and upon the wheels, upon the levers, upon all the apparatus, and you've got to make it stop." And they did.

Their agitation woke up the adults of America, who had meekly been letting the government do their thinking for them. The youth of America listened to voices like that of former Senator Wayne Morse, who declared, "The only hope is that the Nixon policies will result in millions of young people rushing to deliver the message that it is the right and duty of free men to rebel against tyranny."

Dr. Martin Luther King, Jr., also called upon young people to rebel, but by following Mahatma Gandhi's tactic of civil disobedience. "One who breaks an unjust law must do it *openly, lovingly*," he explained, ". . . with a willingness to accept the penalty." He had never felt more a partner in the making of American law, he said, than when he was in jail for breaking it. Thanks to his courage, states which had laws discriminating against blacks were forced by his crusade to change those laws.

Many laws are deliberately broken to test their constitutionality in higher courts. As former Senator Goodell pointed out, some 86 Federal laws and over 700 state and municipal laws have been so challenged and declared unconstitutional by the Supreme Court. Such civil disobedience usually occurs when a number of citizens believe that they cannot change an unjust law by the normal legal processes.

It is important to protect the right of privacy of every citizen from unwarranted spying by government agencies. There are now over 100 different government agencies that have potentially dangerous intelligence functions.

How can we balance a citizen's right to privacy, to be let alone, with the government's need of personal-data banks in order to provide Americans with services and benefits? We need to make certain that access to school records, dossiers and data banks is limited strictly to the purposes for which they were compiled. They must also be open to inspection so that any citizen may challenge and correct any erroneous information about him.

The Freedom of Information Act, passed in 1974, gives you the right to see any Federal records about you, require correction of any inaccuracies and limit the government's use of those records. The ACLU and other citizen groups stand ready to help anyone pursue his or her rights under this law.

There are also private-company data banks that accumulate information which can be requested by government surveillance agencies. Protests to IBM about their personnel files led the company to a startled realization that they had amassed enormous confidential data on employees' private affairs, including health, bank accounts, arrest records and personality traits. IBM decided to stop collecting

162

data on job-application forms which had nothing to do with the company's business.

Sweden has passed a law requiring all commercial data banks to be licensed by a special watchdog board which limits their operation and use. No data bank may list criminal records, psychiatric treatment, alcoholism, political or religious affiliations, or other sensitive matters, except with the board's seldom-granted permission. Individuals may demand to see their files, have all mistakes corrected and sue for damages if misinformation has harmed them in any way.

Business Week noted, "Sweden's new measure, the world's first national data-bank control law, offers a possible precedent and perhaps warning for a U.S. apparently hurtling toward total computerization, amid growing public pressure for protective legislation."

The ACLU lobbied for an expansion of citizens' rights under the Freedom of Information Act. President Gerald Ford vetoed the new bill. The ACLU helped persuade Congress to pass the act over his veto. It then used the law to pry loose government secrets about "shabby things done in the name of national security," such as plotting political assassinations, opening citizens' mail, eavesdropping on their conversations and using people as guinea pigs in experiments with dangerous drugs and diseases.

If we want to stop abuses of our civil liberties, we all have a powerful weapon—the pen. Nothing gets results better than writing letters to our representatives in Congress and our state legislatures, as well as to the press. We can further make our views heard by organizing campaigns that generate letters, articles, editorials and discussions on local TV talk shows.

"In the final analysis it is up to you," states former CIA operative Patrick J. McGarvey. "It is the boom of your voice that will bring about the necessary changes. As an individual you no doubt have a feeling of impotence when it comes to influencing your government. Collectively, however, you have a tremendous impact. It requires only that you get a slight ground swell started."

As an example, in 1976 the protest of just four men was able to delay a government plan to build new nuclear plants that had no foolproof safeguards in many parts of the country. Three General

Electric nuclear engineers and a safety inspector from the Nuclear Regulatory Commission quit their jobs simultaneously, in well-publicized resignations calling attention to the danger of nuclear accidents. The Sierra Club, consumer organizations, the National Council of Churches, the Union of Concerned Scientists and other organizations were galvanized into supporting the protest. The government was forced to suspend its plans indefinitely.

The task of protecting our democracy is not simple. The temptations for those in power to reach for still greater power are enormous. As Lord Acton noted, "Power tends to corrupt and absolute power corrupts absolutely." With the advantage of modern mass communications, notably TV, radio and press, would-be dictators have powerful tools for making people think what they want them to think, believe what they want them to believe.

When you become aware of the government's attempt to manipulate you by using mass communication in this way, it is important that you resist by demanding to hear the opposition. If the President or any other government official makes what you consider a political or biased appeal in the media, you can insist by phone or letter that equal time or space be given to a political opponent to reply. You won't always succeed. But if enough people do it often enough, the media will be forced to stop one-sided government propaganda.

We need to be on guard against government attempts to pass laws that threaten our civil liberties, or to use government agencies to harass citizens, in the name of fighting crime or "national security." A secret FBI memo, exposed in Congressional hearings, revealed that many FBI activities were undertaken to alarm political dissenters into stopping their opposition to government policies out of fear that "there is an FBI agent behind every mailbox." How different was this from the Cheka aim, explained by a Soviet official, "that the mere mention of its name will make everybody abandon any idea of sabotage, extortion or conspiracy"?

We need law, certainly. But we also need liberty. Law without liberty makes a police state. Liberty without law creates anarchy. Law *with* liberty represents the true democracy our forefathers intended us to enjoy.

Democracy is a delicately balanced, fragile construction that can easily be destroyed by citizen apathy. By people who don't bother to vote, shrugging, "What difference does my vote make anyhow?" Or, "Politicians are all crooks anyhow—one's as bad as another." Because of such attitudes, our nation has one of the poorest voting records of any democracy. Too often we get the kind of public officials our disinterest deserves. And we blame them instead of ourselves. Richard Nixon was elected in 1968 by a margin of one vote per election precinct—*every* vote counts!

Albert Speer, Hitler's Minister for Armament and War Production, who was convicted at the Nuremberg Trials as a war criminal, later repented. After being released from prison, he warned Americans in 1976, "It might all happen again unless we are on guard against it."

Michael Scammell, editor of the *London Index on Censorship*, declared, "If one had to draw up a table of freedom of expression around the world, I think America would be at the top. Watergate was the proof of that. But Watergate was also the proof that there are no grounds for complacency."

"Americans are not passive under their faults," noted historian Barbara Tuchman. "We expose them and combat them. Somewhere every day some group is fighting a public abuse—openly and, on the whole, notwithstanding the FBI, with confidence in the First Amendment. The U.S. has slid a long way from the original idea . . . [but] it still offers a greater opportunity for social happiness, that is to say, for well-being combined with individual freedom and initiative, than is likely elsewhere. . . . If the great question, whether it is still possible to reconcile democracy with social order and individual liberty, is to find a positive answer, it will be here."

9

Nevertheless those who have experienced life in a police state warn Americans not to underestimate the danger of losing their freedom, or the suffering that would follow.

"Is it possible or impossible to transmit the experience of those who have suffered to those who have not suffered?" asked Aleksandr Solzhenitsyn, the celebrated Soviet author who had spent years in

Stalin's prison camps. "Is it ever possible to warn anyone of oncoming danger? How many witnesses have come to your country, how many waves of immigration, all warning you of the same experiences and the same dangers? Yet these proud skyscrapers still stand, and you go on believing that it will not happen here. Only when it happens to you will you know it is true."

There is further food for thought in the admission made by Cicero on the fall of the ancient Roman Republic. "It was our own moral failure," he wrote, "and not any accident of chance, that while preserving the appearance of the Republic we lost its reality."

What we can learn from the police state experience of most of the other countries discussed in this book is to some extent limited, because few had the long traditions of political freedom such as we have had. Yet we need to remember that even the oldest democracy in the world, Greece, was transformed into a tyrannical police state as recently as 1967, and suffered under it for over six nightmare years.

Yes, a police state *could* happen here.

But not if enough informed Americans are aware of dictatorial threats and developments early enough, and unite to prevent any erosion of the Constitution and the Bill of Rights.

At our Constitutional Convention in Philadelphia in 1787, where the delegates met in closed sessions, Benjamin Franklin warned them, "This experiment too shall certainly end in despotism when the people become so corrupted that they are incapable of any other form of experiment."

After the Constitution had been adopted to preserve both law and liberty in the United States, Franklin was approached by a woman outside the hall eager to learn how the delegates had voted. "Which is it, Dr. Franklin," she asked, "the Republic or a monarchy?"

"A republic, citizen," he replied. Then as he strode by he added, "If you can keep it."

Bibliography and Recommended Reading

For easy reference the bibliography below is listed alphabetically according to the part of the book to which it especially pertains. Asterisks in front of authors' names indicate books I recommend for further reading. A dagger (†) indicates an author who espouses a viewpoint different from mine, whom readers may wish to consult for themselves. In the bibliography for Chapters V and VI, I have also indicated after each title, where necessary or appropriate, the country which is the subject of the book. For the record I have also listed some of the newspapers and periodicals which have also been sources of reference.

I and VII

*Agee, Philip. *Inside the Company: CIA Diary.* N.Y.: Simon & Schuster, 1975.

†Alger, Bruce, ed. *Revolutionary Actions . . . U.S.A.* Washington: Citizens Evaluation Institute, 1971.

Archer, Jules. *Battlefield President.* N.Y.: Messner, 1967.

*———. *The Dictators.* N.Y.: Hawthorn, 1967.

*———. *The Extremists.* N.Y.: Hawthorn, 1969.

*———. *1968: Year of Crisis.* N.Y.: Messner, 1971.

*———. *The Plot to Seize the White House.* N.Y.: Hawthorn, 1973.

*———. *Resistance.* Philadelphia: Macrae Smith, 1973.

*———. *Revolution in Our Time.* N.Y.: Messner, 1971.

*———. *Riot!* N.Y.: Hawthorn, 1974.

*———. *Treason in America.* N.Y.: Hawthorn, 1971.

*———. *Watergate: America in Crisis.* N.Y.: Crowell, 1975.

———. *World Citizen: Woodrow Wilson.* N.Y.: Messner, 1967.

Arendt, Hannah. *Crises of the Republic.* N.Y.: Harcourt, 1972.

———. *The Origins of Totalitarianism.* N.Y.: Harcourt, 1973.

*Brenton, Myron. *The Privacy Invaders.* N.Y.: Fawcett, 1964.

Brock, William R. *The Evolution of American Democracy.* N.Y.: Dial, 1970.

Chommie, John C. *The Internal Revenue Service.* N.Y.: Praeger, 1970.

Cobban, Alfred. *The Nation State and National Self-Determination.* N.Y.: Crowell, 1969.

*Cogley, John. *Report on Blacklisting.* Santa Barbara, Calif.: Fund for the Republic, 1956.

(Rockefeller) Commission on CIA Activities Within the United States. *Report to the President.* Washington: G.P.O., 1975.

*Committee on Foreign Relations, U.S. Senate. *Warrantless Wiretapping and Electronic Surveillance—1974.* Washington: G.P.O., 1974.

*Committee on Government Operations, U.S. House of Representatives. *Access to Records.* Washington: G.P.O., 1974.

Committee on Internal Security, U.S. House of Representatives. *Terrorism.* Washington: G.P.O., 1974.

Conkin, Paul K. *FDR and the Origins of the Welfare State.* N.Y.: Crowell, 1934.

*Cook, Fred J. *The FBI Nobody Knows.* N.Y.: Pyramid, 1965.

*Cowan, Paul, Nick Egleson and Nat Hentoff. *State Secrets.* N.Y.: Holt, 1974.

*Douglas, William O. *The Right of the People.* N.Y.: Arena, 1972.

*†Dulles, Allen. *The Craft of Intelligence.* N.Y.: Harper, 1963.

*Forster, Arnold and Benjamin R. Epstein. *Danger on the Right.* N.Y.: Random House, 1964.

*Gellhorn, Martha. *The Face of War.* N.Y.: Simon & Schuster, 1959.

*Goodell, Charles. *Political Prisoners in America.* N.Y.: Random House, 1973.

Gorer, Geoffrey. *The Danger of Equality.* London: Cresset, 1966.

*Gregory, Dick. *Dick Gregory's Political Primer.* N.Y.: Harper, 1972.

*Grodzins, Morton. *The Loyal and the Disloyal.* Chicago: University of Chicago, 1956.

*†Hoover, J. Edgar. *Masters of Deceit.* N.Y.: Pocket Books, 1967.

*Houghton, Neal D., ed. *Struggle Against History.* N.Y.: Washington Square, 1968.

Kahn, E.J., Jr. *Fraud.* N.Y.: Harper, 1973.

Kalb, Marvin and Bernard. *Kissinger.* N.Y.: Dell, 1975.

*Kanfer, Stefan. *A Journal of the Plague Years.* N.Y.: Atheneum, 1973.

*Kirkpatrick, Lyman B., Jr. *The U.S. Intelligence Community.* N.Y.: Hill & Wang, 1973.

*Long, Senator Edward V. *The Intruders.* N.Y.: Praeger, 1967.

*Marchetti, Victor and John D. Marks. *The CIA and the Cult of Intelligence.* N.Y.: Dell, 1974.

*Markmann, Charles Lam. *The Noblest Cry.* N.Y.: St. Martin's, 1965.

*McGarvey, Patrick J. *CIA: The Myth and the Madness.* N.Y.: Saturday Review Press, 1972.

*Miller, Arthur R. *The Assault on Privacy.* Ann Arbor: University of Michigan, 1971.

*Mollenhoff, Clark R., ed. *The Pentagon.* New York: Putnam's, 1967.

†Nehemkis, Peter. *Latin America: Myth and Reality.* N.Y.: NAL, 1966.

*Neier, Aryeh. *Dossier: The Secret Files THEY Keep On YOU.* N.Y.: Stein and Day, 1975.

*Nelson, Jack and Ronald J. Ostrow. *The FBI and the Berrigans.* N.Y.: Coward, McCann, 1972.

*Newberry, Mike. *The Yahoos.* New York: Marzani and Munsell, 1964.

*O'Neil, Robert M. *The Price of Dependency.* N.Y.: Dutton, 1970.

*Orwell, George. *Animal Farm.* N.Y.: Harcourt, 1946.

*————. *Nineteen Eighty-Four.* N.Y.: NAL, 1971.

*†Overstreet, Harry and Bonaro. *The FBI in Our Open Society.* N.Y.: Norton, 1969.

Reader's Digest. *Secrets & Spies.* Pleasantville, N.Y.: Reader's Digest Assn., 1964.

Rees, John. *Equality.* N.Y.: Praeger, 1972.

*Rubenstein, Richard E. *Left Turn.* Boston: Little, Brown, 1973.

*Seldes, George. *1000 Americans.* N.Y.: Boni & Gaer, 1947.

*————. *You Can't Print That!* Garden City, N.Y.: Garden City Publishing, 1929.

*Shannon, David A., ed. *The Great Depression.* Englewood Cliffs, N.J.: Prentice-Hall, 1960.

*Szulc, Tad. *Compulsive Spy.* N.Y.: Viking, 1974.

*Thompson, Hunter S. *Fear and Loathing: On the Campaign Trail '72.* San Francisco: Straight Arrow, 1973.

*Tingsten, Herbert. *The Problem of Democracy.* Totowa, N.J.: Bedminster, 1965.

————. *The Swedish Social Democrats.* Totowa, N.J.: Bedminster, 1973.

*Wheeler, Harvey. *Democracy in a Revolutionary Era.* Santa Barbara, Cal.: Center for the Study of Democratic Institutions, 1968.

†Widener, Alice. *Teachers of Destruction.* Washington: Citizens Evaluation Institute, 1970.

*Wise, David and Thomas B. Ross. *The Espionage Establishment.* N.Y.: Random House, 1967.

*————. *The Invisible Government.* N.Y.: Bantam, 1964.

II: Hitler's Germany

*Bleuel, Hans Peter. *Sex and Society in Nazi Germany.* Philadelphia: Lippincott, 1973.

*Blond, George. *The Death of Hitler's Germany.* N.Y.: Macmillan, 1954.

*Crankshaw, Edward. *Gestapo.* N.Y.: Pyramid, 1957.

†Doenitz, Admiral Karl. *Memoirs.* Cleveland: World, 1959.

Gerber, Albert B. *The Life of Adolf Hitler.* Philadelphia: Mercury, 1961.

†Goerlitz, Walter. *History of the German General Staff: 1657–1945.* N.Y.: Praeger, 1953.

*†Hitler, Adolf. *Mein Kampf (My Battle).* Boston: Houghton Mifflin, 1933.

*March, Tony, ed. *Darkness Over Europe.* Chicago: Rand McNally, 1969.

Orlow, Dietrich. *The Nazis in the Balkans.* Pittsburgh: University of Pittsburgh, 1968.

*Shirer, William L. *The Rise and Fall of the Third Reich.* N.Y.: Simon & Schuster, 1960.

Trevor-Roper, Hugh R. *The Last Days of Hitler.* N.Y.: Macmillan, 1947.

*Zuckmayer, Carl. *A Part of Myself.* N.Y.: Harcourt, 1970.

III: Police State, Russian Style

*Archer, Jules. *Man of Steel: Joseph Stalin.* N.Y.: Messner, 1965.

*_____. *The Russians and the Americans.* N.Y.: Hawthorn, 1975.

*_____. *Trotsky: World Revolutionary.* N.Y.: Messner, 1973.

Barghoorn, Frederick C. *The Soviet Image of the United States.* N.Y.: Harcourt, 1950.

*Bonavia, David. *Fat Sasha and the Urban Guerilla.* N.Y.: Atheneum, 1973.

*Dedijer, Vladimir. *The Battle Stalin Lost.* N.Y.: Viking, 1971.

*Douglas, William O. *Russian Journey.* Garden City, N.Y.: Doubleday, 1956.

*Gunther, John. *Inside Russia Today.* N.Y.: Harper, 1962.

*Jacoby, Susan. *Moscow Conversations.* N.Y.: Coward, McCann, 1972.

*Levytsky, Boris. *The Uses of Terror.* N.Y.: Coward, McCann, 1972.

*Litvinov, Pavel. *The Trial of the Four.* N.Y.: Viking, 1972.

†Novosti Press. *Lenin's Ideas Transform the World.* Moscow: Novosti, undated.

*Rositzke, Harry. *The USSR Today.* N.Y.: John Day, 1972.

*Rossif, Frederic and Madeleine Chapsal. *Portrait of a Revolution.* Boston: Little, Brown, 1969.

†Spolansky, Jacob. *The Communist Trail in America.* N.Y.: Macmillan, 1951.

*St. George, George. *Our Soviet Sister.* Washington: Robert B. Luce, 1973.

*Thayer, Charles W. and the Editors of *Life. Russia.* N.Y.: Time, Inc., 1963.

IV: The Chinese Way

*Archer, Jules. *China in the Twentieth Century.* N.Y.: Macmillan, 1974.

*_____. *The Chinese and the Americans.* N.Y.: Hawthorn, 1976.

*_____. *Chou En-lai.* N.Y.: Hawthorn, 1973.

*_____. *Mao Tse-tung.* N.Y.: Hawthorn, 1972.

Bloodworth, Judy and Dennis. *Heirs Apparent.* N.Y.: Farrar, Straus, 1973.

*Committee of Concerned Asian Scholars. *China! Inside the People's Republic.* N.Y.: Bantam, 1972.

*Davies, John Paton, Jr. *Dragon by the Tail.* N.Y.: Norton, 1972.

*Forman, Harrison. *Report from Red China.* N.Y.: Holt, 1945.

*Galbraith, John Kenneth. *A China Passage.* Boston: Houghton Mifflin, 1973.

Harbert, Mary Ann. *Captivity.* N.Y.: Delacorte, 1973.

*Hunter, Deirdre and Neale, eds. *We the Chinese.* N.Y.: Praeger, 1972.

*Myrdal, Jan and Gun Kessel. *Chinese Journey.* Boston: Beacon, 1965.

*Robottom, John. *China in Revolution.* N.Y.: McGraw-Hill, 1969.

*Roy, Jules. *Journey Through China.* London: Faber, 1967.

*Schurmann, Franz and Orville Schell. *Communist China.* N.Y.: Random House, 1967.

*Trumbull, Robert. *This Is Communist China.* N.Y.: McKay, 1968.

*†Tung Chi-Ping and Humphrey Evans. *The Thought Revolution.* N.Y.: Coward, McCann, 1966.

V: Variations on the Left

Aguilar, Luis E. *Cuba 1933.* Ithaca, N.Y.: Cornell University Press, 1972.

*Appel, Benjamin. *With Many Voices* (Eastern Europe). N.Y.: Morrow, 1963.

*Archer, Jules. *Red Rebel: Tito of Yugoslavia.* N.Y.: Messner, 1968.

*_____. *Thorn in Our Flesh: Castro's Cuba.* N.Y.: Cowles, 1970.

*Baring, Arnulf. *Uprising in East Germany: June 17, 1953.* Ithaca, N.Y.: Cornell University Press, 1972.

Brown, J.F. *Bulgaria Under Communist Rule.* N.Y.: Praeger, 1970.

*del Vayo, Julio Alvarez. *Give Me Combat.* Boston: Little, Brown, 1973.

Heikal, Mohamed Hassanein. *The Cairo Documents* (Yugoslavia). Garden City, N.Y.: Doubleday, 1973.

*Holm, Hans Axel. *The Other Germans* (East Germany). N.Y.: Pantheon, 1970.

Landauer, Carl. *Germany: Illusions and Dilemmas.* N.Y.: Harcourt, 1969.

*Langer, William L., et al. *Western Civilization*, Vol. 2. N.Y.: Harper, 1975.

*Matthews, Herbert L. *Revolution in Cuba.* N.Y.: Scribner's, 1975.

*Mikes, George. *Any Souvenirs?* (Eastern Europe). Boston: Gambit, 1972.

*Reckford, Barry. *Does Fidel Eat More Than Your Father?* (Cuba). N.Y.: Praeger, 1971.

*Salomon, Michel. *Prague Notebook* (Czechoslovakia). Boston: Little, Brown, 1971.

Schwartz, Harry. *Eastern Europe in the Soviet Shadow.* N.Y.: John Day, 1972.

†Wolfe, Bertram D. *Communist Totalitarianism.* Boston: Beacon, 1956.

*Zeman, Z. A. *Prague Spring* (Czechoslovakia). N.Y.: Hill & Wang, 1969.

VI: Variations on the Right

*Archer, Jules. *Twentieth-Century Caesar: Benito Mussolini.* N.Y.: Messner, 1964.

Arevalo, Juan Jose. *Anti-Kommunism in Latin America.* N.Y.: Lyle Stuart, 1963.

*"Athenian." *Inside the Colonels' Greece.* N.Y.: Norton, 1972.

*Blanshard, Paul. *Freedom and Catholic Power in Spain and Portugal.* Boston: Beacon, 1962.

*Clogg, Richard and George Yannopoulos. *Greece Under Military Rule.* N.Y.: Basic Books, 1972.

†Coles, S.F.A. *Franco of Spain.* London: Spearman, 1955.

Ferguson, J. Halcro. *The Revolutions of Latin America.* London: Thames and Hudson, 1963.

*Gunther, John. *Inside South America.* N.Y.: Harper, 1967.

*Payne, Robert, ed. *The Civil War in Spain, 1936–1939.* N.Y.: Fawcett, 1962.

*Sampson, Anthony. *The Sovereign State of ITT* (Chile). N.Y.: Fawcett, 1974.

*Schuddekopf, Otto-Ernst. *Revolutions of Our Time: Fascism.* N.Y.: Praeger, 1973.

*Tannenbaum, Edward R. *The Fascist Experience* (Mussolini Italy). N.Y.: Basic Books, 1972.

†Trythall, J.W.D. *El Caudillo* (Franco Spain). N.Y.: McGraw-Hill, 1970.

*Werstein, Irving. *The Cruel Years* (Franco Spain). N.Y.: Messner, 1969.

Woolf, Stuart J., ed. *European Fascism.* N.Y.: Random House, 1969.

Consulted for research were also *The Atlantic Monthly, Center Magazine, Center Report, Changing Times, Civil Liberties, Library of Congress Research Service, CounterSpy, Foreign Affairs, Free China Weekly, Harper's, Ms., The Nation, Newsweek, New York, New York Civil Liberties,* New York *Post, The New York Times, The New Yorker, South African Scope, U.S. News and World Report,* and *Variety.* Material was also obtained from the American Civil Liberties Union, Amnesty International, Committee for a Free China, and Participatión de la Liberación Dominicana.

Index

Central Intelligence Agency (CIA): and anti-Vietnam War movement, 152; attempts assassination of Castro, 94, 154; domestic espionage by, 149–150; illegal acts of, 2; and junta in Chile, 127; warlike acts of, 154

CHAOS, CIA program, 150

Cheka (Soviet secret police), 41; vs. FBI, 164; set up, 38

Chetniks vs. Yugoslav Partisans, 102

Chiang Ching, 78

Chiang Kai-shek, 65, 66, 67; driven out of China, 69; U.S. support of against Mao, 68–69

Chile, police state in, 128–129

China: civil war in, 68–69; collectives in, 70, 74; Communist state developed in, 8, 69–71; cultural life in, 83–84; and Cultural Revolution, 76–77; education in, 80–81; evaluation of, 88–90; and experiment in changing human nature, 70–71; and Great Leap Forward, 74–76; Hundred Flowers campaign in, 74; Japanese invasion of, 66; justice in, 87–88; Kuomintang in, 65–66, 67; labor camps in, 86; and Long March, 66; minorities in, 83; peasants in, 64–65; reconstruction in, 72; regimentation in, 72, 79; and U.S. support of Chiang against Mao, 68–69; workers in, 81–82

Chou En-lai, 66

Church, Frank, 154

Churchill, Winston, 92

Chu Teh, 67

Cicero, 166

Citizens' Committee to Investigate the FBI, 153

Citizens' Defense, Germany, 13

Civil liberties: Chinese view of, 89; suspension of in Nazi Germany (1933), 20; under U.S. Constitution and Bill of Rights, 3–5

Civil war: in China, 68–69; in Russia, 41–42; in Spain, 121–122

Coexistence, peaceful, 48

Cold war, 48

Collectives: in China, 70, 74; in Soviet Union, 53; in Yugoslavia, 104

Colson, Charles, 152

Commager, Henry Steele, 3

Committee for the Defense of the Revolution (Cuba), 97

Committee to Reelect the President (CRP), 155, 156

Communist state. *See* Police state

Communist Totalitarianism (B. D. Wolfe), 51

Concentration camps in Nazi Germany, 30–31

Constantine, King (Greece), 131, 132

Constitution, U.S.: and Bill of Rights, 3–4; guarantees under, 4–5

Council of People's Commissars (Soviet Union), 37

Cuba: Castro takes power, 93–94; Communist state in, 93–101; cultural programs in, 99; Soviet support for Castro, 95

Cuban National Congress on Education and Culture, 99

176

House Un-American Activities Committee (HUAC), 146, 147
Hua Kuo-feng, 78
Humphrey, Hubert, 128
Hundred Flowers campaign (China), 74
Hungary, Communist state in, 108–109
Husak, Gustav, 111
Hutchins, Robert M., 9

Illiteracy. *See* Education
Impeachment hearings on Richard Nixon, House Judiciary Committee, 157, 158
India, police state in, 135–138
Intellectuals: Soviet harassment of, 48; underestimation of Hitler, 32
Internal Revenue Service and tax audits of Nixon "enemies," 155
International Telephone and Telegraph Corp. (ITT) and police state in Chile, 126–127
Ioannides, Demetrius, 134
Iron curtain, 92
Italy, Fascist state in, 8, 115–120

Japan, invasion of China, 66
Jefferson, Thomas, 139, 140
Jenkins, Loren, 136
Jews: deprived of German citizenship in Nazi Germany, 25; as Hitler's scapegoats, 22, 23; in Soviet Union, 55–56
Johnson, Lyndon, and Vietnam War, 150
Juan Carlos, King (Spain), 125
Jurney, Dorothy, 81

Kádár, János, 109
Karamanlis, Constantine, 134
Kent State University (Ohio), students killed at, 152
Kerenski, Aleksandr, and Russian Provisional Government, 36–37
Khrushchev, Nikita: apologizes to Yugoslavs, 105; and de-Stalinization movement, 47; and peaceful coexistence, 48
King, Martin Luther, Jr., 161
Kissinger, Henry, and police state in Chile, 127
Kohout, Pavel, 111
Kornilov, Lavr, 36
Kraft, Joseph, 2
Kronstadt naval base (Russia), 36; sailors' revolt, 42
Krupp, Gustav, 19
Kulaks, liquidated by Stalin, 44
Kuomintang, 65–66, 67

Labor: in China, 81–82; compulsory, of Soviet youth, 50; in Cuba, 97–98; productivity, Chinese, 75; in Soviet Union, 52–23
Labor camps: in China, 86; in Soviet Union, 44, 45, 47
Land nationalization, Russian, 38. *See also* Collectives
Lenin, Nicolai, 8, 9; arrest ordered, 36; and civil war, 41–42; and Russian Revolution, 37–38
Ley, Robert, 22, 26
Liberation Daily (Yenan), 68
Li Cheng-fu, 85
Li Hsien-nien, 85–86
Lincoln, Abraham, and suspension of habeas corpus, 140–142
Lindqvist, Sven, 85

Liu Shao-ch'i, 77

Long March, Chinese Communists', 66

Loyalty Order (U.S.), 146

Loyalty probes in U.S., 146–148

Lumumba, Patrice, 154

Lyon, Matthew, 140

Lysenko, Trofim D., 51

MacGuire, Gerald C., 145

Mann, Thomas, 147

Mao Tse-tung, 8, 9, 66; appeals for U.S. support rejected, 68; and collective farming, 74; and Cultural Revolution, 76–77; and Hundred Flowers campaign, 74; and revelations about Stalin, 73

Marahrens, Bishop, 26

Marchais, Georges, 92

Marx, Karl, 8, 9

Matteotti, Giacomo, assassination of, 117

Matthews, Herbert, 100

McCarran Act (1950), 147–148

McCarthy, Joseph, 147–148

McCord, James, 156

McCormack, John W., 146

McGarvey, Patrick J., 163

Medical care. *See* Health and medical care

Medvedev, Zhordes, 58

Mein Kampf (Hitler), 13–14, 33

MERRIMAC, CIA program, 150

Mihajlović, Draža, 102

Milligan, ex parte, 142

Mitchell, John, 153, 155

Morse, Wayne, 156, 161

Mosley, Sir Oswald, 113

Moynihan, Daniel Patrick, 9

Mussolini, Benito, 8, 9; and Fascist state in Italy, 115–120; as model for Hitler, 12; reaction to German treatment of Jews, 23

Myers, Gustavus, 148

Narodna Mladezh, 112

Nation, 8

National Council of Churches (U.S.), 164

National Education Association (U.S.), 147

National Health Congress (China, 1950), 72

National Party Congress (Russia), 39, 40

National Socialist German Workers' (Nazi) party, 12; and election of 1932, 18; growth, late 1920's, 14–15

National Student Association (U.S.), 153

Nazi party. *See* National Socialist German Workers' party

Nehru, Jawaharlal, 124

New Economic Policy (NEP), Russia, 43

New Labor Front (Nazi Germany), 22

Newspapers in Soviet Union, 56–57. *See also* Censorship

Nicholas, Tsar, 35

Niemoeller, Martin, 33

Nitti, Francesco Saverio, 114

Nixon, Richard M.: and anti-Vietnam War movement, 151–152; and "criminal" presidency, 1–2; impeachment hearings, 157; "imperial" presidency, 159; margin of election victory, 165; and police state in Chile, 127; resigns, 158; and secret police force, 152; tapes, 157; and Watergate affair, 154–158

Novotny, Antonin, 109, 110

Nuclear Regulatory Commission (U.S.), 164

Nuremberg Laws (Nazi Germany, 1935), 25

Okhrana (Russian secret police), 35

Orwell, George, 92

Padilla, Herberto, 101

Palmer, A. Mitchell, and raids on aliens in U.S., 143–145

Papadopoulos, George, and police state in Greece, 131–134

Papandreou, Andreas, 131

Papandreou, George, 130–131, 134

Papen, Franz von: coalition with Hitler, 18; named Germany's Chancellor, 17; reaction to Nazi regime, 23, 32

Pareto, Vilfredo, 8

Partisans vs. Yugoslav Chetniks, 102

Pasternak, Boris, 59

Paton, Lori, 151

Peasants, Chinese, 64–65

Penal code (Nazi Germany, 1935), 24

People's Liberation Army (PLA), China, 70

People's Revolutionary Vanguard (VPR), 130

Peter, King (Yugoslavia), 101–102

Petrograd Soviet, and Russian Revolution, 36–37

Picasso, Pablo, 122

Pinochet Ugarte, Augusto, 128

Plumbers, and Watergate affair, 155–156

Police state (*see also* China; Germany; Soviet Union): in Brazil, 129–130; in Bulgaria, 112; in Chile, 128–129; in Cuba, 93–101; in Czechoslovakia, 109–112; vs. democracy, 5; development of, 8–9; in East Germany, 107–108; in Greece, 130–134; in Hungary, 108–109; in India, 135–138; in Italy, 115–120; in Spain, 122–126; in Uruguay, 126; in Yugoslavia, 101–106

Politburo, Russia, 39

Popov, Aleksandr, 51

Prague uprising. *See* Czechoslovakia

Privacy vs. data banks in U.S., 162–163

Propaganda: Chinese, 71; Nazi (1930's), 15, 22–23

Provisional Government of Russia (1917), 36–37

Purges of Soviet Communists, 44–45

Rather, Dan, 152

Rauff, Walter, 128

Ray, A. N., 137

Reconstruction, China, 72

Red Army, China, 66–67

Regimentation, China, 72, 79

Reichstag (German parliament): and Enabling Act, 21, 32; fire, 32; Goering becomes presiding officer, 18; Nazi seats in, 15

Religion: Cuba, 99; and failure of

Religion, *continued*
Nazi Germany's spiritual leaders, 33; Nazi attacks on, 26; in Soviet Union, 56
RESISTANCE, CIA program, 150
Revolts: Czechoslovakia, 48, 110, 111; East Germany, 107; Hungary, 109; Kronstadt sailors', 42
Revolution in Cuba (Matthews), 100
Roehm, Ernst, 17; and Storm Troopers, 23–24
Roosevelt, Franklin D., 25, 145, 159
Roy, Jules, 84
Rozing, Boris, 51
Rubin, Vitaly, 55–56
Russia (*see also* Soviet Union): Provisional Government set up (1917), 36; Provisional Government overthrown, 37; Revolution, 36–37; Tsar abdicates, 35–36; World War I unrest, 35, 37

Santayana, George, 139
Savio, Mario, 161
Scammell, Michael, 138, 165
Schleicher, Kurt von, 18, 24
Schlesinger, Arthur, 159
Secret police: Cheka, 38, 41, 164; Chile, 128; Greece, 132; Nixon, 152; Okhrana, 35; Soviet, 47, 57; Yugoslavia, 106
Security index, FBI, 153
Sedition Act (1917), 142, 143
Senate Watergate Committee, 156, 157
Service, John S., 68
Sforza, Count Carlo, 116

Sierra Club, 164
Skolenko, A. G., 53
Snow, Edgar, 90
Socialist Workers party, FBI break-ins of, 149
Social Revolutionary party (Russia), 36
Solzhenitsyn, Aleksandr I., 61, 165
Soviet of Workers' and Soldiers' Deputies, 36
Soviet Union (*see also* Russia): agricultural worker in, 52–53; civil war (1921), 41–42; development of Communist state in, 8; dissidents in, 58–60; education in, 47, 49–51; factors in becoming police state, 62–63; factory worker in, 52; and help for Chinese Communists, 72; Jews in, 55–56; and Kronstadt sailors' revolt, 42; nationalization of land, 38; New Economic Policy (NEP), 43; power pyramid in, 39–40; secret-police power curtailed in, 47; and support for Castro, 95; taxes in, 53; women in, 38–39, 54
Spain, 121–126; Basque separatist movement, 124–125; civil war, 121–122; Fascist state in, 122–126
Speer, Albert, 165
Stalin, Joseph, 9; crimes exposed, 47; "excommunicates" Yugoslavia, 104–105; feud with Tito, 102–103; Five-Year Plans, 44; liquidates kulaks, 44; succeeds Lenin, 43–44; as World War II leader, 46
Steffens, Lincoln, 41
Stolar family, 56

Storm Troopers, Nazi Germany: brutality, 22; and Hitler's putsch, 13; under Roehm, 23–24; suppressed, then restored to uniform, 17

Strength Through Joy Association (Nazi Germany), 28

Sturua, Melor G., 56

Suárez, Adolfo, 125

Sun Yatsen, 65, 66

Taxes: in Fascist Italy, 116; in Soviet Union, 53

Terrill, Ross, 79

Thought control, in China, 72–73

Tibet, Chinese control in, 83

Tito, Josip Broz: brand of Communism, 105–106; feud with Stalin, 102–103

Trotsky, Leon: exile and murder, 44; and Russian Revolution, 36, 37

Trujillo, Rafael, 154

Truman, Harry, and loyalty probes, 146–148

Tuchman, Barbara, 165

Ulbricht, Walter, 107

Underground newspapers, Soviet, 57

Unemployment: in Chile, 128; in Germany (1930), 15; Nazi solution to, 26–27

Union of Concerned Scientists, 164

Union of Soviet Socialist Republics (USSR). *See* Soviet Union

Uruguay, police state in, 126

Van der Lubbe, Martin, 20

Versailles Treaty, 11

Vietnam War, dissent on, 150–154

Vittorio Emanuele III, King (Italy), 114, 116

The Washington Post, 155, 156

Watergate affair, 154–158

Weicker, Lowell, 153, 154, 156, 158

Weimar Republic (Germany), 11; failure of, 31; and Hitler's putsch, 13

Welfare state, in Cuba, 98

Wicker, Tom, 136

White House Plumbers and Watergate affair, 155–156

White House tapes, 157

Wilson, Woodrow, 10, 41; and police-state tactics, 142–144

Wirth, Joseph, 32

Wolfe, Bertram D., 51

Women: in China, 82–83; in Fascist Spain, 123–124; in Soviet Union, 38–39, 54

Woodward, Bob, 155

Workers. *See* Labor

World War I, unrest in Russia during, 35, 37

Writers, Soviet, 59–60

Yao Wen-yuan, 88

Yuan Shih-k'ai, 65

Yugoslavia: "excommunicated" by Stalin, 104–105; Hitler's invasion of, 101–102

Zuckmayer, Carl, 32

Format by Gloria Bressler
Set in 11 pt. Times Roman
Composed, printed and bound by The Haddon Craftsmen, Scranton, Penna.
HARPER & ROW, PUBLISHERS, INCORPORATED